THE NON-ELECTRIC LIGHTING SERIES

BOOK 7: Propane for Preppers

Ron Brown

Newark Valley, New York

Text and photographs by Ronald B. Brown.

Cover by FK.

Copyright © 2015 by Ronald B. Brown. All rights reserved. No part of this publication may be reproduced, stored in a retrieval system, or transmitted in any form by any means, electronic, mechanical, photocopying, recording, or otherwise without the prior written permission of the copyright holder, except brief quotations used in a review.

Notice: This manual is designed to provide information on propane gas and propane-fueled lamps and appliances.

It is not the purpose of this guide to reprint all the information that is otherwise available, but to complement, amplify, and supplement other texts and resources. You are urged to read all the available material and learn as much as you can about propane and to tailor the information to your specific circumstances.

Every effort has been made to make this guide as complete and accurate as possible. However, there may be mistakes, both typographical and in content. Therefore this text should be used only as a general guide and not as the ultimate source of propane information. Furthermore, this guide contains information that is current only up to the printing date.

The purpose of this manual is to educate and entertain. The views, opinions, positions, and strategies expressed by the author are his alone. The author makes no representations as to the accuracy, completeness, correctness, suitability, or validity of any information in this book and will not be liable for any errors, omissions, or delays in this information or any losses, injuries, or damages arising from its use.

ISBN 978-0-9970228-0-3

Published by R&C Publishing
15 Dr. Knapp Road South
Newark Valley, NY 13811

Printed in the United States of America

Table of Contents

PART ONE 11
Introduction 11

Safety 13

Chemistry 14

Adapters & Substitutions 21

MAPP Gas 28

Selected Reader Comments, Part One 30

PART TWO 33
Plumbing 33

Conclusion to Part Two 45

Selected Reader Comments, Part Two 45

PART THREE 53
The Economics of Refilling 53

Legalities 54

Leakage 55

So Here's How You Do the Doin' 57

Selected Reader Comments, Part Three 69

PART FOUR 74
Refilling a 20-Pounder 74

Storage of One-Pounders 77

Carbon Monoxide 82

Oxygen Starvation 85

Selected Reader Comments, Part Four 86

PART FIVE 91

Carbon Monoxide Revisited 91

What Are the Risks Surrounding Propane? 96

Inhaling Propane Vapors 96

Oxygen Starvation 97

Inhaling the Products of Combustion 98

Product Warnings 102

Extinguishing a Propane Fire 103

The Rest of the Story 104

Dangers of Overfilling 106

Purging 109

Safety (and the double standard thereof) 111

Disposal of Empty Propane Cylinders 113

Selected Reader Comments, Part Five 115

FOREWORD

Having sufficient fuel for lighting, cooking, and heat following an emergency is always a concern for preppers. I say this because if the stuff hits the fan, many, if not most of us, will turn to propane as a primary fuel source.

That being said, the only experience many of us have with propane is limited to the backyard barbecue and perhaps a Coleman lantern. That tells me many of us are woefully lacking in the knowledge necessary to use propane efficiently and safely.

This book, written by my friend Ron Brown, will fix that. So how did this book come about?

It began as a series of articles written exclusively for my blog _Backdoor Survival_ (http://www.backdoorsurvival.com). In that sequence, Ron took considerable time to put together a comprehensive tutorial for my readers with a focus on safety.

To say that the series was well received is an understatement. Today, _Propane for Preppers_ is one of half a dozen items I keep tucked away under a tab entitled "The Best of Backdoor Survival." It was, and is, that good.

My guess is that Ron agreed to write the series because he planned a 'propane book' as part of his Non-Electric Lighting Series. I am glad he did, because as it turns out, this book, _Propane for Preppers_, not only includes a reprint of the Backdoor Survival series, but also includes additional material gleaned from the more interesting comments and questions posed by Backdoor Survival readers.

Here is a synopsis of the parts:

Part One explains safety, chemistry, adaptors, and substitutions. It teaches a bit of terminology and how the manufacturers themselves describe their products (e.g. is it a canister, a cylinder, or a cartridge?). This information is invaluable in providing clues on what to search for online or ask for in a hardware store.

Part Two moves on to the nitty gritty of tanks, valves, and regulators. It includes a discussion of the whys and wherefores of using propane. There is considerable detail relative to the safety concerns we should be on the watch for while using propane. This includes leaks, poor fittings, and heaven forbid, an old tank with blue fittings indicating the tank was once used to produce crystal meth.

Part Three explains how to refill the ubiquitous one-pound cylinders that are used with portable lanterns, stoves, and heaters. There are pros and cons to doing this, mostly relating to safety considerations – no surprise there. If you are not mechanically inclined and do not have an outside area in which to work, refilling one-pound propane tanks may not be for you. The last thing I want, after all, is for you to blow yourself up along with the rest of the neighborhood!

Part Four discusses the long-tern storage of one-pounders, introduces the topics of carbon monoxide poisoning and oxygen starvation, and describes the refilling of 20-pounders (the kind of propane tank used on BBQ grills). Frankly, on the topic of refilling 20-pounders (not to be confused with the little one-pounders), Ron scared me off completely. He suggests, and I couldn't agree more, that before you undertake the refilling of a 20-pounder, you have a heart-to-heart with your fire insurance agent. Enough said.

Part Five is the final installment. It expands upon carbon monoxide plus discusses propane fires, the dangers of overfilling, purging new cylinders, disposing of empty one-pounders, and finally, the rather strange double standard that seemingly exists in the universe of propane safety.

As with all things preparedness, knowledge is power and with Ron's help, learning to safely use and store propane will surely help us make it through a future "disruptive event."

Be well and be safe!

Gaye Levy
Backdoor Survival
2015

"Let there be light . . ." (Genesis 1:3

PART ONE

Introduction

This has been a difficult series of articles to write. The word 'prepper' covers a lot of territory.

Whether it's a blackout or a race riot – and both have occurred in these United States during my lifetime – what's the plan? Shelter in place? But is that a single-family dwelling with a cellar? Or a one-bedroom apartment on the 17th floor?

Or is 'the plan' to get outta Dodge? On foot? Bicycle? Motorcycle? Car? And where will you go? To a relative with a spare bedroom? Hunting camp? Boat? RV?

Not only is the audience hard to pin down, propane (the subject of this article) is so versatile that it's hard to know where to begin.

You can convert your automobile to run on propane. And the outboard motor on your boat. And your motorcycle. And your lawnmower. And your electric generator. My sister has a backup system, a generator that runs on propane, which will support most of the electrical needs in her home – including the electric range in the kitchen. Every Friday night her lights flicker as the system goes into its weekly self-test.

There are refrigerators that run on propane. Little ones for RV's and big ones for full-time off-grid living. Not to mention furnaces and space heaters (both vented and unvented) and catalytic heaters, plus gas lamps, water heaters (with tanks and without), air conditioners (absorption chillers, by any other name, that work on the same principle as gas refrigerators), fireplaces, clothes dryers, kitchen stoves for cooking, salamanders for the construction site to keep the freshly poured concrete from freezing, and toilets.

Yes, toilets. If your land has poor drainage, you can install a gas-fired toilet that will incinerate human waste after each deposit thereof.

So which prepper am I talking to? The single gal living with her grandmother on the 17th floor? Or the survivalist with more ammo than he can carry? And what are the topics I should cover? I just now discovered an adapter, for example, a wand-like tube with a fitting on one end, that converts an old-time Coleman liquid-fuel camp stove to propane. And another adapter that allows you to run a BBQ grill from a little 400-gram Bernzomatic soldering cylinder. And another that will let you hook up *natural gas* devices to propane.

OMG. It hurts my head to think so much.

Safety

Safety is a good place to start. *Safe-mindedness.*

Propane has been sold commercially since the 1920's. A lot of safety features have been engineered into propane devices – the storage tanks, for example, as well as BBQ grills and camping gear. It's best to not bypass these features. Let me give you an example.

Today, propane tanks are made such that they can't be filled more than 80%. When 'full' the bottom of the tank contains liquid propane and the top 20% of the tank contains propane in the gaseous state. *Gas* can be compressed. *Liquid* cannot. If you bypass this safety feature and fill the tank 100% and leave it out in the sun, heat will make the liquid expand. First the blowout plug (a fuse of sorts) will go. If the blowout hole cannot accommodate the volume of propane trying to escape, the tank will burst, creating a propane cloud. A mere spark can ignite the propane cloud, sending both you and your propane tank to join all the computer files you previously sent to 'the cloud.'

There's a lot of Attitude out and about. "Nobody's gonna tell me what to do." It's a control issue. I get it. But you might want to make an exception when it comes to propane. Just this one time you might want to consider following the rules.

Call it food for thought on your trip to the hospital.

Chemistry

Crude oil is the stuff that gets pumped out of the ground. Crude oil is refined into a whole range of products from gases (propane, butane) to liquids (gasoline, kerosene) to solids (paraffin wax).

All of these products are hydrocarbons. The 'hydro' part of the word stands for hydrogen (symbol = H). The 'carbon' part of the word stands for carbon (symbol = C). Am I going too fast?

In refining, distillation breaks or fractures the crude oil into groups of hydrocarbons with similar boiling points. The five major fractions are (1) refinery gases, (2) gasoline, (3) kerosene, (4) diesel oil, and (5) residues.

Our interest here is in the first group, refinery gases. And there are four: methane, ethane, propane, and butane.

The refinery gases have the following chemical formulas: Methane is C_1H_4. Ethane is C_2H_6. Propane is C_3H_8. Butane is C_4H_{10}. This is simply a reference list. Sometimes we need to be precise in our language so as to remove any confusion regarding which gas is under discussion.

Note that the C-number or carbon-chain number climbs one step at a time throughout the progression: $C_1 - C_2 - C_3 - C_4$.

The English language can be ambiguous. The word 'gas' has several meanings: [1] it can mean gasoline (petrol to the British), or it can mean [2] methane or propane ("Now you're cooking with gas."), or it can mean [3] a vapor (as in the three states of matter – solid, liquid, and gas), or it can be [4] a euphemism for farting ("He passed gas."). As we go along I'll do my best to make the meaning clear.

Methane (C_1H_4). Methane is used as a fuel, commonly called natural gas, and is transported via pipeline in LNG form (liquefied natural gas). Methane is also the swamp gas of UFO lore. Methane is lighter than air.

Lamps that burn natural gas inside your home, common in the gay '90s – the 1890's – back when 'gay' meant happy – are still manufactured today. Paulin, Mr Heater, and Humphrey are three U.S. brands. Their use requires that you have a natural gas line into your house. If you heat with natural gas, you do. Lamps burning natural gas are wall-mounted (or ceiling-mounted) and thus not portable. Note that such lamps can readily be converted to propane.

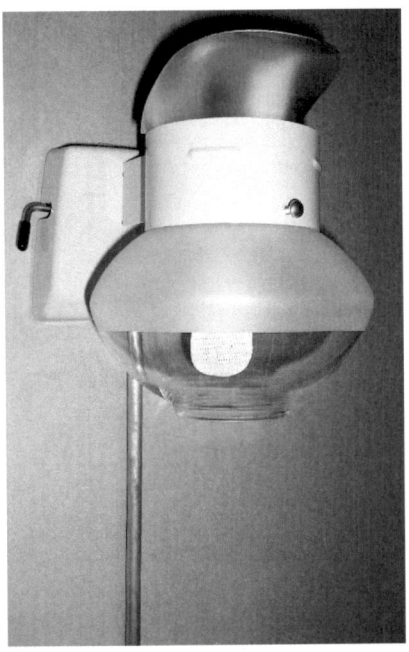

If you put in one of these wall-mounted lamps (and, personally, I think it's a great idea to do so), I urge you to have it installed by a certified-licensed-authorized technician and not attempt the installation yourself.

Should you ever have a house fire, the insurance company will look for excuses not to pay. So let's not void our fire insurance to save a few bucks on installation, shall we?

Ethane (C_2H_6). Ethane is used as a catalyst in other chemical processes, moreso than as a fuel in and of itself.

Propane (C_3H_8). I live in the country, beyond the reach of natural gas pipelines. As a consequence, I have a 200 lb. propane tank behind the house. We use propane for cooking.

The company who delivers our gas is Suburban Propane. I can drive to their storefront and refill a small 20 lb. cylinder to use on a camper or RV (recreational vehicle) or propane BBQ grill. The tank behind my house and the 20 lb. cylinder contain exactly the same stuff – LPG (liquefied petroleum gas).

The skinny little propane cylinders sold for Bernzomatic (brand) soldering torches hold 14.1 oz. (400 grams). The more squat 'one-pounders' sold for camping stoves and lanterns, hold 16.4 oz. (465 grams). That's how much they hold. *What* they hold is LPG. That is, propane. That is, C_3H_8. Propane is propane is propane.

Can you hook up a propane camping lantern, the kind that customarily runs on a one-pounder, to a 20 lb. propane tank? Sure. The fittings and extension hoses to do so are sold as a kit under the Century brand name. And the Mr Heater brand name. And the Coleman brand name. I bought one myself in the camping section at Walmart.

Wall-mounted propane gas lamps (and other appliances such as refrigerators) are often employed in cottages and hunting camps located at a distance from both electricity and in-town natural gas lines. These appliances burn LPG (liquefied petroleum gas) rather than LNG (liquefied natural gas).

LPG and LNG lamps can look identical on the outside but propane is more highly pressurized. Propane lamps therefore use a nozzle with a smaller orifice (the hole through which the gas comes) than do natural gas lamps. If you move from city to country, or vice-versa, your gas clothes dryer presents exactly the same orifice problem. Fortunately, conversion kits are readily available.

Propane, by the way, is heavier than air. It pools in your basement. And it pools in the hull of your boat; it only takes one spark to cut your vacation short. Check out 'boat explosions' on YouTube. It will likely make you sit up and take notice. It did me.

Butane (C_4H_{10}) Like propane, butane is also heavier than air. Please note that we are still climbing the C-numbers.

It's interesting that, given the right adapters, *propane* can be substituted in camping lanterns and stove burners originally designed for butane. It's not just theory. I've done it. You can too.

Most butane cigarette lighters are disposable; some are refillable. If refillable, you'll find a small fitting on the bottom of the lighter. Note that the butane cartridge must be turned upside down to fill the cigarette lighter. In your hands, you can feel the butane cartridge get cold as the transfer of gas takes place.

Butane is used in cigarette lighters, in pressurized cartridges for one-burner stoves, and in camping lanterns for backpackers. It turns from a gas to a liquid at 31° F (almost the same as the freezing point of water).

Mexico has a warm climate and butane, they say, is favored over propane as cooking gas. Butane is even called 'Mexican gas.' Google will reveal many images of large (100-pound) butane tanks.

In cities with a large Asian population (e.g. Toronto, Canada), one-burner stoves that run on butane cartridges are for sale in all the ethnic food stores. I've also seen them on eBay and in restaurant supply stores (caterers use them). The fuel cartridges are lightweight, similar to shaving cream containers. They hold 8 ounces (227 grams).

These butane stoves are a pleasure to use – easy to light, regulate, and extinguish. Why they're not more popular with the state-park-camping crowd is no doubt their low-temperature limitations. Ditto for the use of butane in lanterns. Below freezing, a lantern that runs on butane (and there are some) will not light. How wonderful is that? (FYI, I've seen lanterns that run on these 8-ounce butane cartridges under the brand names of Kovea, Glowmaster, and American Camper.)

Adapters & Substitutions

American Camper sells (1) a butane-only lantern as well as (2) a Multi Fuel Lantern that comes with an adapter; it will run on either the 8-ounce butane cartridges or propane one-pounders.

It is interesting, is it not, that propane (C_3) can, given the right adapter, be burned in the same appliance that uses methane (C_1). A clothes dryer, for example. At the other end of the spectrum, propane (C_3) can be burned in the same appliance that uses butane (C_4). The American Camper lantern, for example.

Mini-lanterns and micro-stoves using butane cartridges (in 110-gram, 230-gram, and 450-gram sizes) are made for backpackers. Unlike the 8-ounce canisters discussed above, the cartridges have a threaded $7/16$" male coupling. (And, typically, they contain a propane-butane blend – to avoid freeze-up – rather than pure butane.)

So wadda ya do when you have a lantern or stove made with the screw-type coupling but only have an 8-ounce cartridge of butane to use as fuel? Come now. That's why God made adapters.

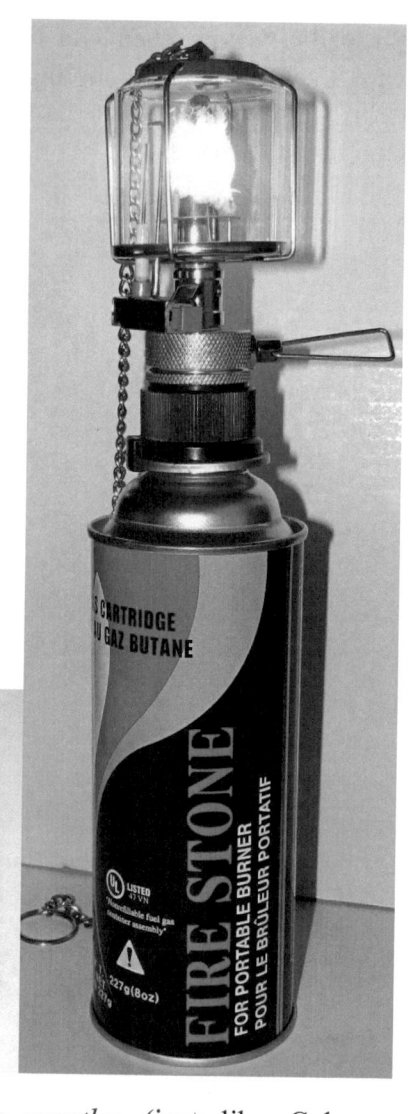

Tip. Butane lanterns use *mantles* (just like Coleman lanterns). Butane lamp instructions (auto-translated from Chinese via computer) typically say 'wicks' or 'gauze.' *Oops!* Sorry. They are *mantles*. Although mantles are beyond the scope of this discussion, it's 'mantles' you need to ask for at the sporting goods store, not wicks or gauze.

Back to our story. Say you have a butane lantern or stove made with the screw-type coupling but you only have a *propane* one-pounder for fuel? Solution. A different adapter. The adapter shown below is the Kovea VA-AD-0701.

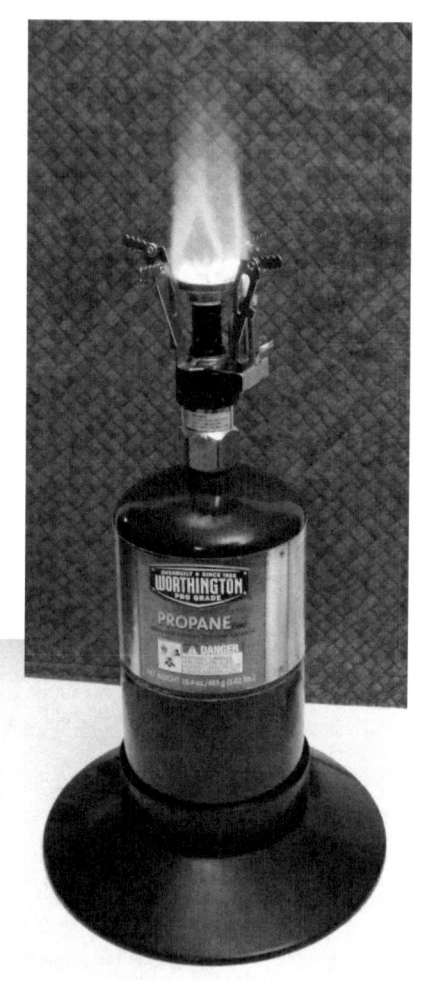

Aside. There's one application for propane one-pounders that I don't much care for. It's the direct-screw-on single-burner stove. To me, it looks awfully top-heavy when loaded with a pot of water. *Boiling* water being sterilized in a grid-down situation. Let's just hope the cat doesn't jump on the table and knock anything over.

Speaking of adapters, you can use an adapter to *refill* a propane one-pounder from a 20-lb. cylinder. That will be covered in Part Three of this series. But before we embark upon the 'how-to' of refilling, we first need to understand some basic plumbing stuff – tanks and valves and such – so that we have our terminology straight. Plus there are safety issues that we need to understand.

MAPP Gas

And even before that, let me mention MAPP gas. MAPP originally stood for **M**ethyl**A**cetylene-**P**ropadiene **P**ropane although today (since 2008) products labeled MAPP are really MAPP substitutes.

Small MAPP 'welding sets' are widely sold. They employ oxygen cylinders as well as MAPP gas cylinders. The MAPP gas cylinders are the same size and have the same threads as the soldering cylinders (Bernzomatic variety) that hold propane.

So let's put MAPP gas in context.

Given the right adapter (and there are several brands of adapters we'll identify when we get to that section in Part Three), we can refill a propane one-pounder.

And, using the same adapter, we can refill the skinny Bernzomatic-type soldering cylinders. The shape of the cylinder is different from a one-pounder but the threads are the same.

And we can refill a MAPP-gas cylinder with propane. Again, the threads are the same so we can use the same adapter. Let us be clear. The MAPP cylinder comes from the store holding MAPP gas. When empty, we can refill it with propane. From a technology point of view, it's no more complicated than storing salt in a sugar canister.

But leave yourself a clear trail. A label on the cylinder would be a good place to start. As an analogy, how good are you at finding stuff on your computer? Stuff that you, yourself, tucked away where you could always find it. So, remembering which gas cylinder it was that you refilled two or three years ago . . . and where you stored it . . . and how you labeled it. "Houston, we have a problem."

Selected Reader Comments, Part One

- **Comment #5.** 'JR' commented:
  I remember back in 1999 when Y2K was all the talk. The knowledgeable preppers were looking for 500 or 1000 gallon propane tanks with a valve on the bottom. It requires a valve on the bottom to be able to get the liquid out of the tank. The top valve gives off the gas. It take liquid to fill the 20 lbs tanks and prepping groups were storing 20 pounders all over the hill sides for the coming bad times. They needed reliable filling stations.

  - 'JS' responded:
    J, an ex-employer of mine refilled his 20# tanks from a 250 gallon tank. The hose connection was on the top of the tank. Apparently there is a pipe under the hose connection that extends down into the tank, allowing the gas pressure to push the liquid propane out the hose.

  - Ron Brown:
    In a later installment we'll describe the refilling of 20-pounders (BBQ-tank size) from bigger tanks. It is doable. That's a fact. But it has the potential to burn down not your house but your neighborhood. That's also a fact. You might want to talk it over with your fire insurance agent before you start.

- **Comment #9.** 'RZ' commented:
  Hope I am not getting ahead of the articles here, but propane electrical power generators are VERY common in the communications business. Propane does not go stale, or decompose when stored for long periods. This makes it perfect for stand-by power at remote sites. Diesel, especially the new Ultra Low Sulfur Diesel fuel (ULSD) can go bad in a matter of months without proper storage. Propane, on the other hand, stays just the way it

was delivered for years. There is that little matter of temperature though, and if you live in cold climates you either run your generator on liquid, taken from the bottom of the tank, or you have tank heaters installed that keep the propane just above the completely liquid level.

- **Comment #12.** 'SN' commented:
Excellent article, Ron. Thanks for the info. Perhaps you can help me . I picked up an old Magic Chef gas stove (circa 1940's) with the intention of brewing beer outdoors with it or actually cooking with it should the need arise. I attached a propane tank and regulator to it but the burners will not stay lit. It looks like the orifices on the elements are too large and are not compatible with the pressure/volume of the propane. My guess is that this unit wants to run on natural gas. Can you explain the difference in the two and recommend a course of action? I really want to get this stove up and running. Thank you!

  - Ron Brown:
  Propane is under higher pressure and the orifice (the hole through which the gas comes) is smaller than it is with natural gas. Your local gas company (i.e. the business or firm who would install a tank and deliver propane to your home) will have a serviceman equipped with conversion kits for clothes dryers and kitchen stoves to switch from natural gas to propane and vice versa. That's where I would go. He'll know what he's looking at. He'll have the tools and parts to fix it.

- **Comment #14.** 'B' commented:
Propane is NOT very efficient to run generators. Not many people realize that. A 20lb tank won't last very long. Gas is still the most efficient. Unless you have one

of those huge "buried" tanks, but propane is still not very efficient, which surprised me.

- **Comment #17.** 'S' commented:
Wow! So much information, good information! I have only recently put my mind to the importance of getting prepared. Articles like this are not only informative but also inspirational. I have alway been a "one step at a time" kind of person and this shows how to get ready step by step.

- Ron Brown:
Thanks. Propane has some features to recommend itself: it's widely available, it can be stored without degrading, and it's available in many container sizes and increments. On the downside, you must use some discretion. I used to teach seminars with a guy who said to the students, "Don't park your brains at the door." I never cared for his phraseology but it sure does apply to propane. You must stay focused. Propane is HIGHLY flammable. One spark can change your life. You think texting-and-driving don't mix? Well.............

PART TWO

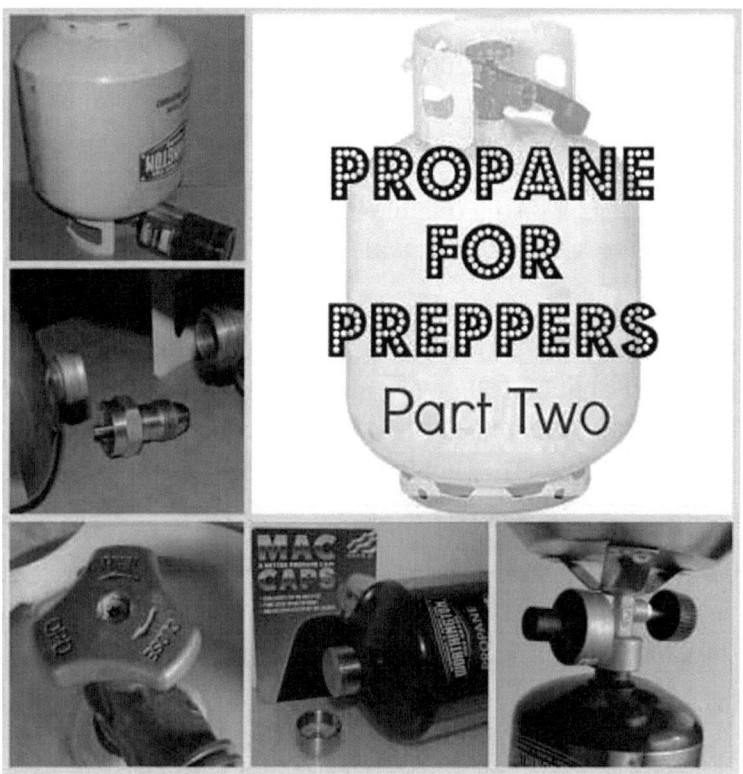

Plumbing

Crystal Meth. Ten years ago I wouldn't have bothered to include this section. Today it's top on the list.

I live in the country, near a village with one stoplight, 30 miles from Walmart. Yesterday, in a house just up the road, there was an explosion that blew the front door off its hinges and the glass out of all the windows. The only person home at the time went to the hospital with burns over 75% of his body. It's the fourth meth bust we've had locally in the past 12 months. As Bob Dylan said in 1964 (50 years ago), the times they are a-changin'.

People who make meth use propane tanks to hold ammonia. The tanks are made of steel but the fittings are made of brass. And ammonia attacks brass, cracks it, and makes it brittle. Makes it *unpredictable*. And it gives the brass fittings a distinctive blue color. The tank may or may not hold pressure without exploding.

Urban legend has it that such tanks are sometimes turned in, refilled, and recycled back to propane customers. Extremely unlikely. For one thing, the tanks are screened by propane suppliers. For another, as Snopes points out, anyone turning in a meth tank (with its prominent blue corrosion) would be drawing attention to himself. A far more likely scenario would be finding such a tank in the garage of the house you just rented, left behind by previous tenants. Or finding one at a flea market. (http://www.snopes.com/crime/warnings/methtank.asp)

If you do come across such a tank (that is, a propane tank where the brass fittings are corroded to a blue or blue-green color), don't move it. You don't know what's inside or how much pressure it's under or how close it is to blowing. Will it take the jostling and jarring of being moved? There's no way to tell. Call the fire department. Let them bring in the bomb squad. Seriously. Don't move the tank yourself.

I don't own such a tank, or even pictures of such a tank, so that I can show you what the blue color looks like. But if you'll Google for 'ammonia blue propane' you'll find lots of images. Check it out. Once you see it, you can't unsee it.

Tanks. Propane tanks come in all sizes. I worked many years at an aluminum mill. We consumed enough gas in the 'soaking pits' to light a small city. Literally. Had a big snowstorm. Blackout. Lost production. Mega-bucks. We installed propane tanks big enough to run for a week without interruption. It looked like a supply depot. It *was* a supply depot.

On the other end of the range are cartridges that hold 110 grams (4 oz.) of a propane-butane blend. Weight-wise, that's equivalent to half a cup of water. A hiker can toss a cartridge into his backpack and not notice the weight. That kind of cartridge is intended to power small lanterns and one-burner stoves.

Within those two extremes, this article will focus on the lower end of the range – one-pounders and 20-pounders for the most part. The one-pounders are made to be disposable, not refillable. Technology-wise, one-pounders can be refilled and adapters to do so are widely sold. Part Three of this article will show you how. But when we do it, we'll be taking on all associated risk. Please be aware.

The skinny (Bernzomatic) soldering cylinders have the same (right-hand) threads that one-pounders have. And that MAPP-gas cylinders have. They can all be refilled the same way. Unfortunately, they are all made to be disposable and they are all prone to leaking. I've had it happen several times. An audible hiss; escaping gas that you cannot stop.

Threaded brass end caps will stop the leak if an O-ring is added. A basin of water with a leaking one-pounder in it reveals a stream of bubbles coming from the valve. If you install a brass end cap, the bubbles continue. If you wrap the threads with Teflon thread-seal tape, the bubbles continue. If you install a gasket cut from a sheet of rubber-cork gasket material from the automotive supply store, the bubbles continue. If, however, you replace the factory-installed gasket with an O-ring ($^{15}/_{16}$" outside diameter) from your local hardware store, the bubbles stop. *Bingo!*

Unfortunately, brass end caps are expensive. An alternate is a propane device that's no longer functional (because it's plugged, dented, etc.) – soldering tips and such that you pick up at yard sales. These devices can be mounted on a one-pounder in place of an end cap. Plus-or-minus an O-ring, they'll stop leaks.

Another way to use a leaky cylinder is to store it (empty) until you need it, then refill it immediately before use. But that means you must leave the appliance attached to the cylinder until the propane is totally consumed. Else the leaking resumes.

Side Note: *Brass* end caps are used because brass is non-sparking. Flint and steel makes sparks. Even steel and steel makes sparks if you bang the pieces together just right. Sparks are a constant threat, a constant fear, around propane. But you can bang on brass all day long and not get any sparks. And that's a good thing, a wonderful thing.

Let's move on up the food chain. The next size larger tank after a one-pounder is a four-pounder. Actually, the so-called 4-pounder is 4¼ lbs. Seems like an odd increment but no doubt it was intended as a 'one-gallon' tank. One gallon of propane weighs 4.23 lbs. at 60° F.

One pounders have right-hand threads, are intended as disposable (not refillable), and lack the 80%-refill safety feature I described at the beginning of this article. All tanks from 4 to 40 lbs. have left-hand threads, *are* refillable, and *do* have the 80%-refill safety feature (called OPD or Overfill Protection Device).

In the 4-lb. to 40-lb. range, tanks made before 1998 lacked OPD. The shutoff knobs on the older tanks had a variety of shapes – round, 5-point star, 6-point star, etc. Those tanks are gone now, retired when their certification dates expired. Plus, since 2002, they could not legally be refilled. They've effectively been bled out of the supply chain and have all but disappeared.

What remains in circulation (in the 4-lb. to 40-lb. range) are tanks with a standardized shutoff knob, triangular in shape and stamped 'OPD'. Not only do OPD tanks have a float inside to prevent over-filling, if the valve is accidentally left open and the tank is not hooked up to anything, no gas comes out. Sweet.

Propane is sold in both pounds and gallons. At the kind of store where you take your tank to be refilled (a feed store, for example, or a home-heating-oil dealer), the unit of measure is *gallons*.

There are also trade-in stations, for lack of a better term, where you turn in your empty tank and return home with a full (and different) tank. At such a station, *pounds* is the unit of measure.

A '20-lb. cylinder' is sized to hold 20 pounds of propane (net) when it is 80% full. So its 'total' capacity (theoretically) is 25 pounds ($20 \div 25 = .80$). But the tank's internal float prevents you from putting more than 20 pounds in it.

The empty or unladen weight of a container is its 'tare weight.' The tare weight of a propane cylinder is stamped on its collar. Pictured below is the collar of a nominal 20-lb. propane cylinder. 'TW' stands for tare weight. In this case, the tare weight is 16.6 lbs. (16 lbs. 10 oz.).

So if you removed this exact tank from your BBQ grill and weighed it, and it weighed 30 lbs., then you'd know it contained 13.4 lbs. of propane (30 − 16.6 = 13.4). And you'd know it contained 67% of its rated 20 lb. capacity (13.4 ÷ 20 = .67).

When this tank is filled to capacity (20 lb.), it will weigh 36.6 lbs. (20 + 16.6 = 36.6). Anything below that indicates underfilling. At the trade-in station where you turn in your empty tank (plus a few bucks) in exchange for a full one, you can weigh your new tank (giving you the gross weight), subtract the stamped tare weight from the gross, and see how much propane, net, is actually in your new tank. So will it be a full 20 lbs.? Or less than 20 lbs.?

Blue Rhino says about itself: "In 2008 . . . Blue Rhino followed the example of other consumer products companies [and] . . . reduced the amount of propane in our tanks from 17 pounds to 15 pounds." (http://www.bluerhino.com/Help/FAQ/Tank-Exchange#FAQLink135)

(Don't be alarmed. This is nothing more nor less than the universal business model in action. After all, I can remember when a pound of coffee weighed 16 ounces instead of twelve. This is what the communications people mean when they say, "The world is getting smaller.")

Refillable tanks are certified for twelve years from the date of manufacture (stamped on the collar). At the end of twelve years they must be tested and recertified. The recertification is good for five additional years.

And how about the disposable one-pounders we want to refill? There is no collar. The date of manufacture is unknown. There is no recertification procedure. Translation. If you refill it, you're on your own. You're assuming all risk, all responsibility. I'm not saying, "Don't do it." But I am saying, "Be careful."

Valves. Some years back, if you cooked with gas, having two 100-lb. tanks with changeover valves was SOP (standard operating procedure). That's what I had as a married student back in the day, supplying my 12' x 60' house trailer. Today, I have a 200-lb. tank owned by the gas company. My gas company waives any rental fee. Some companies charge. When I had 100-lb. tanks, I, myself, transported them to the vendor to get them refilled. Today, with a 200-lb. tank, the vendor sends the truck to me.

About the only place I see changeover valves (sometimes called switchover valves) today is on RV's where they use two 20-lb. tanks. BBQ grills typically have *one* 20-lb. tank.

With changeover valves, when tank #1 gets empty the valve automatically switches to tank #2. At that point you can shut off and remove tank #1, haul it away to get it refilled, and have supper cooking on tank #2 while tank #1 is off-line.

I once stayed with some folks in their travel trailer who had changeover valves but who didn't understand them. Tank #1 ran out of gas. They shut everything off – I failed to convince them it was unnecessary – and, despite the fact that tank #2 was available, supper waited while someone drove to town, many miles on back roads, to fill tank #1. What part of h-u-n-g-r-y don't you understand?

Newer changeover valves (e.g. Extend-A-Stay or Stay-A-While) look different than the old-style valves but perform the same function. If you don't understand how they work, there's no harm in asking your gas supplier. YouTube also has some good tutorials. Search for 'LPG changeover valves.'

Regulators. Regulators are the heart of a propane system. Regulators keep the gas pressure to an appliance constant even though conditions change. Say it's noon and 70° F outside. The pressure inside your propane tank is 145 PSI. You turn on a stove burner (to cook down a big pot of tomatoes from scratch, say) and set the burner on 'medium.' The sun comes out and by 1:00 PM it's 90° F outside. Due to the increase in ambient temperature the pressure in your propane tank rises to 180 PSI.

But the flame at your stove is still 'medium' in size. Then your gas-fired hot water heater starts up. And your gas-fired clothes dryer shuts down. But even with demand bouncing around in addition to the change in tank pressure, the flame under your tomatoes remains 'medium.' Looks like magic to me.

Actually it takes two regulators to perform the magic. One regulator of the type pictured below is mounted on the big tank supplying your home. (The one pictured here even sends a radio signal to the delivery truck saying you need a refill.) In addition, each individual appliance (stove, fireplace, water heater) has its own secondary regulator.

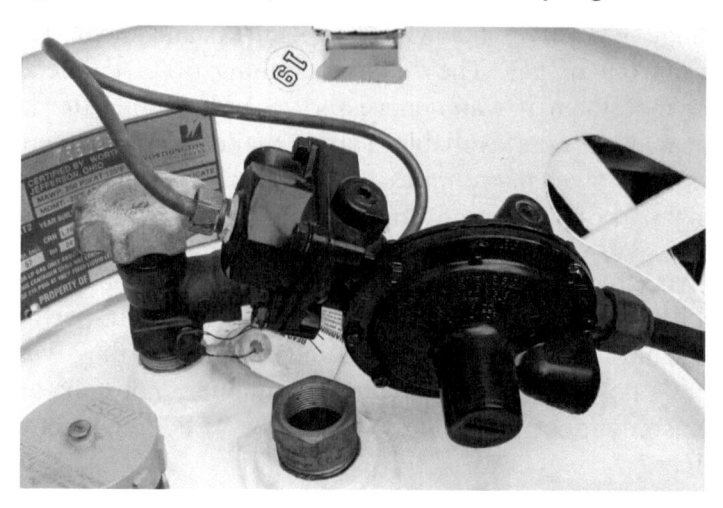

With portable tanks and smaller devices there is only one regulator. Your BBQ grill has its own regulator (the 20-lb. supply tank has none). The one-burner stove that screws onto the top of a one-pound cylinder has a regulator (the one-pound supply cylinder has none). With these smaller devices the regulator is part of the appliance, not part of the fuel supply.

Pipes. The RegO Company (the name is derived from Regulator and Oxygen) has a free, downloadable, 52-page, LP-gas serviceman's manual. It's far more technical than this article but might be nice to tuck away for reference. It's available at http://gameco.com.au/files/24.pdf.

In my house, we have a gas cook stove and a gas clothes dryer. One ½" copper pipe comes from the outside LP tank through the concrete-block wall into the basement and thence to a 'T' coupling. After that, each leg feeds one appliance. Simplicity itself.

Aside. When we bought our house, there was an electric range in the kitchen. We replaced it with propane so that we could cook normally during a blackout. Granted, in a blackout, the stove's electronic sparking system does not spark and we must light the burners with a match. I can handle that.

Back to our story. In a more complex setup – one propane tank feeding several apartments, for example – a manifold system (similar to what you have for water) is used. Such systems have large pipes near the source and progressively smaller pipes as you move further away from the source.

The RegO manual explains how to size such a manifolding system (plus tons of other stuff). More than you ever wanted to know.

Of more immediate concern is the issue (some would say myth) of unshielded copper tubing running through a concrete wall and being corroded by the concrete. To avoid that corrosion, some building codes around the country (not all) require plastic-coated tubing.

I once had an LP-gas serviceman install a new tank, look at the unshielded copper-to-concrete installation already in place, and tell me I needed to change it. He was new to both his company (who had actually performed the installation some years earlier) as well as to the area. He was simply citing the rules and regulations as he knew them from a different section of the country.

It appears that the well-intended serviceman was wrong. Radiant heating systems have had copper tubing buried in concrete for years. I suggest you to check it out yourself. Here's a good place to start:
http://www.plbg.com/forum/read.php?1,438388.

Conclusion to Part Two

The best advice I can give is to learn this stuff now, before you need it. Propane, butane, lanterns, stoves, adapters, refilling, how to tie a mantle on a lantern . . .

Don't just read about it. There's a difference between riding a bicycle and reading about it. Growing vegetables and reading about it. Refilling a propane cylinder and reading about it.

I know several teenage girls who do a fabulous job with nail polish but who are a hazard to both themselves and their surroundings if they attempt to strike a match. They've seen it done. They know it's theoretically possible. But they've never actually done it. *Geeze!* [roll eyes]

Point is, don't wait until the middle of a blackout and the house is cold and the baby is fussy. Get some hands-on experience now – with all these old-timey skills from grandpa's era – before you need them. It will give you confidence, put you in control, give you peace of mind. You'll gain the conviction that you can cope. A good feeling to have.

Okay. I'll stop preaching.

Selected Reader Comments, Part Two

- **Comment #2**. 'h' commented:
  He mentioned yellow Teflon tape for propane,... what if a person uses the white plumbing Teflon tape instead? The white stuff is what my local hardware store recommends, for low pressure devices anyway.
  I don't recall ever seeing yellow tape.

- Ron Brown:

    As far as I know, white Teflon tape is intended for water and yellow for gas. (Plus DuPont holds the Teflon trademark and doesn't like the phrase "Teflon tape" because they, DuPont, no longer make it.) The white tape has been stretched during its manufacturing process. It is both thinner and lower density (more porous) than yellow. For gas, the story I get is that white tape will work; yellow tape will work better. And by all means, don't be afraid to Google for it.

- **Comment #3.** 'JW' commented:

    Ron – I have gotten tanks at the exchange place that, although seeming full, I could get no drop an out of. You said " Not only do OPD tanks have a float inside to prevent over-filling, if the valve is accidentally left open and the tank is not hooked up to anything, no gas comes out. ". Could his be cause by a bad float, or as some people say, because the tank is full of water? If the float, is there anything the average person can do to get it working properly? (35 miles each way is a bit far for returning the tank, especially during an emergency when you need it NOW)

    - Ron Brown:

        If your tank is not hooked up to anything and you open the valve and "can't get a drop out of it," GOOD. That's the way OPD is supposed to work. If, however, your tank is hooked up to an appliance and nothing comes out, different story.

        At the feed store where I get my BBQ tank refilled, there are twenty abandoned OPD tanks at any given time setting in rows near the refill station. Why? Because with the float paraphernalia inside, OPD tanks are more delicate than the old-style tanks they replaced. But the good old boys don't know that. They let the 20-pounders roll around in the back of their pickup trucks just like gramps usta do. Clankity-bump. Eeee-haw!

If the tank/float/valve is at fault and no gas comes out even though it's properly hooked up and you know the tank to be full, then NO, there is nothing the average person can do to fix it. That's why the abandoned tanks are lined up at the feed store.

You might consider testing your new tank right there in the parking lot before making the 35-mile trip home. Doing so would require an adaptor hose plus a small appliance (e.g. camp stove), and those devices are not free, but there is no technological reason why it couldn't be done.

- **Comment #4.** 'D' commented:
This is ONE topic which I've been sadly lacking. Acquired a foldable bbq grill but it's supposed to hook up to propane. (Have patience, all female house w/no male advisers here) lol Anyway, I don't like those small 'throw away' bottles and would like to get a small refillable tank for the car and a standard tank for home. What sizes do I look for? From the reply to JimW, I'm going to be taking my bbq grill when I go buy these babies too. ☺ Thanks so much for the great article.

  - Ron Brown:
  As far as I know, the smallest size refillable propane tank is the 4.25 lb. (one gallon) size. If you Google for it ("4.25 lb. propane tank") you'll find that Lowe's and Home Depot and several other stores carry it. The "standard tank" you want for home use is likely the 20-pounder. And EVERYBODY sells those. The 20-pounder is what's on everyone's BBQ grill. Ironically,

the little 4.25-pounder is over $50 whereas the bigger (and more popular) 20-pounder is only $30. Say what?

With the 20-pounders, there are places you can trade in your old, empty tank (plus a few bucks) and take home a different, full tank. It's quick. You don't have to hang around waiting for somebody to fill your tank. To get started on this swap system, you can outright purchase a filled tank.

OR you can start out by buying a new, empty tank AND GET IT PURGED and filled, then keep taking the same tank back for refilling. With a 4.25-pounder, this second option is your only choice. The first option (turn-in-an-empty-and-go-away-with-a-full-but-different tank) can only be done with 20-pounders. (Although TIAEAGAWAFBDT has a nice ring to it, don't you think?)

- **Comment #5.** 'h' commented:
  Thanks for the unexpected reply.
  The question I now face is: should I, or shouldn't I, replace the tape on the connections for the propane/generator/conversion set-up?
  ... I'm going with: maybe later, but get some yellow to have on hand, especially for the brass elbows.
  - Ron Brown said:
    As far as I know, the "Teflon" part of the Teflon tape is the same, be it white or yellow. It's not like propane will dissolve the white tape or anything like that. It's just that the yellow tape, being slightly thicker and slightly less porous, will contain or confine GASEOUS propane better than will white tape. White tape will suffice with a LIQUID, but a gas, under pressure, is more easily contained with the heavier yellow tape.

That being said, if the joints you already have don't leak . . . then they don't leak. Check them out with soapy water. If they don't leak . . . well, what more can you ask of them?

- **Comment** 7. 'K' commented:
Ron (?), regarding "purging" ; If I purchase a NEW 20# propane tank (from Walmart for instance) do I need to inform the guy at the propane station that it's new and needs purging ? If "yes", does that mean that I then need to pay for the tank to be filled and emptied 4 times before I take it home ??
Thanks..........K

- 'JW' commented:
K – the purging is done with gas (vapor), not liquid. After purging then the tank is filled with liquid. So, I don't think you would be charged much if any for the purging. I do admit that I haven't had that experience, but I would probably argue if they tried to charge me for "filling" it 4 times! Maybe a small additional charge for labor, but not for "filling".

- Ron Brown:
The guy at the propane station will likely notice that the tank looks brand new and ask you if it has ever been filled. But don't take the chance. You tell him right up front. I have never been charged for purging and would be surprised if anyone did so. To the propane company, it's part of the cost of doing business. The cost of purging the occasional tank (filling it with GAS and venting it to the atmosphere 4 times) is built into the day-to-day propane price. You'll be back for a refill. They'll get you then. Don't worry; they're not giving anything away.

- **Comment #8.** 'TM' commented:
Ron
you say "the issue (some would say myth) of unshielded copper tubing running through a concrete wall and being corroded by the concrete"....

Here in UK most houses have central heating systems where the wall mounted radiators are fed by copper pipes through which the water heated by the boiler circulates. On the ground floor these pipes sometimes have to be run under the cement floor to get to each radiator so as to avoid 'unsightly' runs of pipe along the walls which then are often boxed to hide them. The practice is to sheath the copper pipes in plastic, though its not thick stuff, more like freezer bag thickness. The pipes of course have water flowing through them, not propane gas. What I wanted however to point out is that if that sheathing is broken you can indeed get corrosion and 'pinhole' size leaks. We have had that happen three times in our house, and always at the point where a copper pipe is emerging from the floor, which is the point, for aesthetic reasons I guess, where the sheathing stops. The only solution is to smash the surface tile, dig out the cement until you are down to undamaged copper pipe and make good with a joint and a decently sheathed piece of new pipe. I've learnt the hard way to take the precaution of watching the installer like a hawk and insisting on thicker plastic sheathing, e.g. damp proof course thickness which I've purchased myself, being wrapped several times round the replacement pipe and joint until it stands proud of the floor by a few millimetres. The place the leaks occur haven't had someone with a foor mop making them wet, nor has the joint above onto the radiator itself leaked back down the pipe and onto the floor. In two cases the floor round the pipe was carpeted. So any external moisture would purely be from the air. It takes many many years for copper pipe to corrode usually in these circumstances, but plumbers here always say it is because of something in the cement that the corrosion eventually occurs if unsheathed.

- Ron Brown:
  Glancing back over your remarks, I'm reminded of wooden fence posts that rot off at ground level. Fence posts don't rot off down in the ground. The rot is always at the interface of soil and air. Same thing?

- **Comment #10.** 'J' commented:
Sir:

I have had some difficulty obtaining clear information regarding the fuel that stores best in large tanks, such as a 500 gallon tank. I have looked at diesel, bio-fuel, propane, and gas. However, my preference is to use bio-fuel, since it is the only alternative fuel that allows me to produce myself with my own processor and crops, in the event of any catastrophe that interrupts supplies that must be provided by others. If biofuel can be stored for a reasonable period of time, it will affect my decisions regarding the cars I drive and the generator I buy for my home and outbuildings. Your thoughts please.

- Ron Brown:

  J, at its best, bio-fuel offers you, the individual, the possibility of being energy independent on an ongoing basis. It's a control issue, no? Bio-fuel would allow YOU to be in control of your own destiny.

  But does bio-fuel give the biggest bang for the buck where land use is concerned? You'd be converting (1) acreage to (2) corn to (3) ethanol to (4) miles driven. Is that a better return than (1) acreage to (2) corn to (3) cash to (4) gasoline to (5) miles driven?

  Will you really be energy "independent?" Or will your DEpendence simply shift from Mobil to Mother

Nature. Drought and floods and swarms of bugs come to mind.

Health. When you get old and can't do it any longer. To whom do you pass the baton?

On a macro scale, we already use 10 petroleum calories to produce one food calorie. If we reverse the process, how many food calories will we consume in the production of one petrol-equivalent calorie?

We have drifted off-topic here, haven't we?

PART THREE

The Economics of Refilling

A store-bought one-pounder is double or triple the cost of a home-filled cylinder.

My propane supplier just now filled our 200-pound tank behind the house. He charged $3.86 per gallon including 3% sales tax. A gallon of propane weighs 4.23 lb. so my propane cost $.91 per pound (3.86 ÷ 4.23 = .91).

A so-called 'one-pounder' holds 16.4 ounces (465 grams) or 1.025 pounds (16.4 ÷ 16 = 1.025).

Using these figures, were I to home-fill a propane one-pounder, it would cost $.93 per cylinder (.91 x 1.025 = .93).

Walmart's lowest-priced one-pounders are $2.90 per cylinder including 8% sales tax.

On this basis, store-bought cylinders are triple the cost of home-filled cylinders (2.90 ÷ .93 = 3.12).

But here's a worst-case scenario. Another dealer, locally, charges a flat $12 (including sales tax) to refill a 20-pounder, be it empty or almost full. In other words, he's topping it off for $12.

If you reserve a 20-pounder exclusively for refilling and always top it off when it gets down to 50%, then you're effectively paying $1.20 per lb. Even so, if you do the arithmetic, it works out that a store-bought one-pounder is more than double the cost of home refilling.

Legalities

All the propane one-pounder brands I've seen (currently on the market in the USA) carry this disclaimer on the label: "Never refill this cylinder. Federal law forbids transportation if refilled – penalty up to $500,000 and 5 years imprisonment (49 U.S.C. 5124)."

Coleman's statement is even stronger: "Never refill this cylinder. Refilling may cause explosion. Federal law forbids . . . blah, blah, blah." The explosion bit does not appear on other brands.

Coleman one-pounders sold in Canada and Coleman one-pounders circa 1980 carry softer warnings. In Canada the label says, "Do not refill cylinder." NEVER is replaced with 'do not.' And there is no mention of explosion. The old 1980 label says, "It is HAZARDOUS TO REFILL this cylinder." [emphasis theirs] Quite different from NEVER. And, again, no mention in 1980 of explosion.

In the business world, these are classic CYA statements (Cover Your Fanny). The propane company doesn't care if you refill the cylinder. They just don't want to get hauled into court. So to escape any legal liability they say, "Never refill . . ." That gets them off the hook.

U.S.C. stands for United States Code; '49' is the chapter. You can Google for it. And then argue all day about what it means. Does it apply only to 'commerce' and not to private individuals? As a federal law, does it apply only to interstate transportation across state lines? Or does it apply to intrastate transportation as well?

The 49 U.S.C. 5124 statement even appears on Coleman-Canada propane labels. I assume its function is to scare people. I don't see where it would have any more relevance in Canada than the Canadian age of consent has in the USA. (Raised in 2008, BTW, from fourteen to sixteen.)

Transportation notwithstanding, I strongly doubt it is a crime to REFILL a propane cylinder. If it were, then Mr Heater and MacCoupler and EZ Adapters and CE Compass and Gascru and Schnozzle (all of which are brands of refill adapters) would be accessories. As would Amazon, eBay, and your local hardware store where the adapters are sold.

Leakage

Cylinder leakage is a legitimate concern.

One-pounders have a Schrader valve as their main valve. A Schrader valve is what you have in your car or bicycle tire. The Schrader valve seat, the seal, is rubber.

Bigger tanks (such as the 20-pounder we'll use as a source-tank in refilling), employ brass needle valves. Big difference in reliability and life expectancy.

When you attach and detach a one-pounder to an appliance (stove, lantern, etc.) gaseous propane travels through the cylinder's Schrader valve. When you refill, liquid propane travels through the valve. I'm not sure if that does any harm but I'm certain it lacks any benefit.

Of course, the sporting-goods company wants you to throw out the old cylinder and buy new. As discussed in Part One, brass end caps with O-rings will stop a cylinder from leaking. But if you don't test the cylinder after refilling, and if you don't install a brass end cap plus O-ring on the leakers, you'll be traveling down the road wafting a trail of gaseous propane behind you, extremely flammable stuff.

As the old saying has it, "Your right to swing your fist ends with the beginning of my nose." Rephrased: "Your right to travel the highway with a leaking propane cylinder ends just before you blow up me and my family."

Curiosity got the best of me and I cut the top off a one-pounder. You can see the bottom end of the main Schrader valve and a reverse Schrader valve, for lack of a better term, that serves as the cylinder's pressure-relief valve. The relief valve appears upper-left in the image; it's barely visible on the outside of the cylinder but inside it is bigger than the main valve.

As discussed in an earlier installment, one-pounders are prone to leaking. I've had it happen several times. Please don't casually dismiss the possibility.

So Here's How You Do the Doin'

First, to paraphrase Mark Twain, there are two kinds of men. Those who learn by reading the directions. And all the rest of us who must pee on the electric fence and find out the hard way. So let's get to it.

1. Materials. We need (1) an empty one-pounder, (2) an adapter, and (3) a 20-pounder at least half full.

We also need (4) an insulated sleeve to slip over the one-pounder and (5) a brass pushpin, discussed below, with which to release pressure from the one-pounder.

(6) Leather gloves are a good idea to avoid frostbite if something goes wrong. As are (7) safety goggles. Frostbitten fingers are one thing; frostbitten corneas (should you get hit in the face with a blast of liquid propane), quite another.

2. Environment. We need a heavy-duty table (like a picnic table) to work on. Being outside, a 'floor' of blacktop or concrete would be welcome. We don't need a table-leg to sink into mud or soft dirt and dump our tanks on the ground. Oops.

It is imperative to work outside where there is good air circulation (to disperse any puff of propane that may escape as we screw and unscrew cylinders). And to disperse a 'propane cloud' should the unthinkable occur.

In 2012, Stanley Johnson (Polk County, Minnesota) had a fatal explosion – it was his wife who died actually, not he – while refilling a one-pounder inside his garage. Propane is heavier than air. It pools on the floor. Outside, Stanley would have had a fire. Inside, he had an explosion.

3. Procedure. Turn the 20-pound supply-tank upside down. The valve where (liquid) propane will exit is then at the bottom. Inside the tank, liquid propane is immediately above the valve. Gaseous propane is at the top, next to what is now the ceiling of the tank.

4. Screw the adapter into the supply-tank. This is tricky spot #1 because we're dealing with a left-hand thread (meaning that, when tightening, it turns counter-clockwise, contrary to ordinary nuts-and-bolts). We snug the adapter tight with a 1⅛" open-end wrench. 'Snug' is all we need. It's the adapter's rubber O-ring that forms the seal.

5. Screw the one-pounder, the receiving-tank, into the other end of the adapter. (Note that we're starting with the supply-tank and the receiving-tank at the same temperature.) When attaching the one-pounder, it's the old "righty-tighty, lefty-loosey" because we're dealing with an ordinary right-hand thread.

But it's really tricky spot #2. Why? Because one end of the adapter has a left-hand thread and the other end has a right-hand thread. If we over-tighten the receiving-end we simultaneously loosen the supply-end. My solution is to leave the open-end wrench in place to serve as a handle. It's then easy to prevent loosening the adapter from the supply-tank. The wrench can be removed when we no longer need a handle.

6. Once the tanks are hooked firmly together, remove the handle/wrench, tip the supply-tank up on its side (slightly)

to gain access to its triangular valve-knob, then reach under there and open the valve full.

7. Wait one minute for the filling to complete. You can hear a hissing noise (for 10-30 seconds) as the transfer takes place but I've found that one minute gives better results than ending the fill right after the hissing stops. Five minutes, on the other hand, does not give better results than one minute.

8. Turn off the triangular valve-knob and remove the newly-filled one-pounder. This is tricky spot #3. Turn off the supply-tank before unscrewing the receiving-tank. I really need to impress this upon you. DO NOT REMOVE THE ONE-POUNDER BEFORE YOU TURN OFF THE 20-POUNDER.

Although I just said it three different ways, one forgetful moment will reward you with a propane cloud – generated by liquid propane, under pressure, gushing out of the 20-pounder. A propane cloud has the potential for a major fire or explosion. One spark at considerable distance – your neighbor lighting his BBQ grill, for example – can do the trick. This is not kid stuff. You are coloring outside the lines here.

I mentioned in an earlier installment that, with today's OPD valves, if no appliance is hooked up to the tank then no propane will exit the tank even if the valve is left open. Great! HOWEVER, when we remove the just-filled one-pounder, the 20-lb. source tank is still hooked up to an appliance: the ADAPTER.

My fear is that, once you see how easy it is to refill a one-pounder, you'll lose respect for any potential danger. Just the other day my wife and I saw a woman walk into a telephone pole – ALMOST – while texting. She was coming towards us on the sidewalk but not really paying attention to what she was doing. She stopped with the pole just six inches from her nose.

We laughed out loud. She was horribly embarrassed. She was so distracted by the phone that she forgot where she was walking. Is that so much different than watching the girls sunbath next door and neglecting to turn off the 20-pounder before we remove the one-pounder? DISASTER!

Refilling is both easy and safe IF you stay focused.

So if we're talking on the cell phone (tucked securely betwixt ear and shoulder) while we do this . . . or we're distracted by the girls sunbathing next door . . . and we neglect to turn off the 20-pounder before we unscrew the one-pounder . . . DISASTER!

Gary Wayne Suggs (Texas) died in 2008 from a 'flash fire' when he attempted to refill a one-pounder. His father sued K-M Products (MacCoupler) for a defective adapter but filed a Motion to Dismiss in 2009. Adapters are pretty rudimentary devices – one piece with no moving parts. Did Gary just forget to turn off the supply tank? The simplest explanation is usually the correct one. But we'll never know. Gary is dead.

This is no more complicated than not opening the driver's door into oncoming traffic or not leaving your kids in an idling car while you visit the ATM or forgetting to turn on your headlights when you pull out of the gas station at night. But people do dumb stuff all the time.

With propane, if you do dumb stuff, you die.

Once you've launched a propane cloud, BTW, reaching into that cloud to turn off the forgotten valve will produce frostbite. Converting from liquid to vapor (and that's what the propane is doing) requires heat. Just like when liquid water turns into gaseous steam, heat is required.

Heat. Calories. Your hand will supply calories. And when your hand gives up calories your hand gets cold. Google for 'frostbitten fingers' and click 'images.' I GUARANTEE it will make an impression.

At this point (assuming you're still alive and all is well), you've detached the one-pounder with 280 grams of propane inside. That's 60% of the one-pounder's 465-gram capacity.

Your results may vary. The 60% figure is 'typical.' I've gotten everything from 54% to 75% using this same procedure and I've given up trying to understand the variance.

9. Next, release some pressure from the receiving-tank (the one-pounder). Do this by pushing in on the one-pounder's Schrader valve, located top-center on the cylinder. It's like letting air out of a tire. Depress the valve-stem for 5-10 seconds.

Do it outside. Hold the one-pounder upright. That will release gaseous propane from the top of the cylinder. Holding the one-pounder upside down will release liquid propane. Not good.

Use a brass rod to depress the Schrader valve. This is important. Brass is non-sparking. A 'lift wire' for use on your flush toilet is just under $1/8$" in diameter plus being brass. Perfect.

MasterPlumber

**Lift Wires
Varillas Elevadoras
Para Pera de
Descarga de W.C.**

In this procedure, you're not really 'releasing pressure' *per se*. Rather, the pressure-release chills the receiving-tank. You can feel in your hands the one-pounder get cold. The colder tank temperature equates to lower pressure inside the tank; pressure varies directly with temperature.

10. Quickly screw the one-pounder back onto the adapter and slide the insulated sleeve over the one-pounder. You just took steps to make the one-pounder cold; now keep it cold.

My insulated sleeve is a homemade cardboard cylinder covered with three layers of bubblewrap. The sleeve's bottom-end was made by winding an inch-wide strip of bubblewrap into a 'wheel' (slightly oversize), then shoehorning the wheel into the hole in the bottom of the cardboard cylinder.

Even before adding the insulated sleeve, there's precious little clearance between the side of the one-pounder and the tabletop. With the sleeve in place, all clearance disappears. Hence the 20-pounder must perch fairly close to the edge of the table so that the one-pounder (and sleeve) can hang completely off the edge.

11. Next, repeat steps #6-8. That is:

    (6) Open the valve on the supply-tank.

    (7) Wait one minute for filling to occur.

    (8) TURN OFF THE SUPPLY TANK, remove the insulated sleeve, and unscrew the receiving-tank.

At this point you can expect your receiving-tank to contain somewhere between 435 and 480 grams net. That's a range from 94% to 103% of the one-pounder's 465-gram capacity. Gee, 100% has a nice ring to it. (Your results may vary)

If you do the chill-thing with the Schrader valve but, in the next step, fail to use an insulated sleeve, you can expect 325-400 grams net in the one-pounder. That's 81% to 86% of its capacity. (Your results may vary.)

So . . . can you use this technique to top off your not-so-well filled one-pounders? That is, can you chill the cylinder via the Schrader valve and then keep the cylinder cold in an insulated sleeve? Can you do that with a one-pounder now filled to 60%, say, and bring it up to 100%? Can you? Yes.

12. Assuming, again, that you are still alive and have survived step #8 (twice), weigh the newly-filled cylinder to check for over-filling.

A brand new one-pounder holds 465 grams net of propane. The tare weight is 400 grams. That's a gross weight of 865 grams or 30.5 ounces. If your cylinder is overfilled, you can burn off the excess with an appliance (stove burner, for example) or keep poking the Schrader valve with your brass rod – psst – until the cylinder is merely full, not overfull. If you use the psst method, do it outside.

In a later installment we'll discuss the dangers of overfilling and the necessity of leaving some headspace in the cylinder. For the moment, please take it on faith that you DO NOT want to overfill any propane cylinder.

13. Immerse your newly filled one-pounder in a basin of water and check it for leaks.

If it blows bubbles from the main valve, you can poke at it with your brass rod and attempt to get the valve seated properly. Do it with the cylinder upright so that gaseous propane escapes, not liquid propane. Failing that (and, to be honest, the brass-rod thing has never worked for me), install a brass end cap plus O-ring as discussed in an earlier section.

If you have no way of capping off a leaker, install it on a stove burner (or other appliance) and run the device until the one-pounder is empty. Do not store propane in a leaking cylinder. You don't need neighbors complaining about the funny smell or the noise of an explosion. You know how picky neighbors can be.

If the one-pounder blows bubbles from the safety valve, don't even try and fix it. Just use up the gas immediately and dispose of the cylinder.

Theoretically you could pull-and-snap-release the stem of the safety valve with needle-nose pliers in an attempt to seat it properly but that's steel-on-steel; non-sparking it ain't. And if you're really aggressive, I've heard tell of people pulling the valve stem right out of the cylinder. Woot, woot!

Yanking the valve stem out of a full one-pounder would constitute a genuine emergency. Should it happen, hold the cylinder upright. If you turn it upside down, liquid propane will surge out; a propane cloud. And let's hope you're outside when it happens. Everything you can think of produces sparks. Electric motors when they start. Light switches. Uncle Harry when he lights his cigar.

But, hey, if the one-pounder is full and doesn't leak and you're still alive and the barn didn't burn down and your nose hairs didn't get singed and you don't have frostbite . . . then you can swagger along home with bragging rights, eh? Plus you saved $1.97. That's my kinda afternoon.

Selected Reader Comments, Part Three

- **Comment #3.** 'A' commented:
  I have done this a few times.
  Put the one pounder cylinders in the freezer for half and hour before refilling them.
  This will close to the 100% fill rate.

  - Ron Brown:
    Thanks for your interest but I strongly recommend AGAINST chilling a one-pounder in the freezer. I have used the freezer method myself and it has always resulted in overfilling. Granted, it's what you'll see most often on YouTube but I personally believe that the people recommending it are wrong. Gas (headspace) in the cylinder can be compressed. Liquid cannot be compressed (not liquid water and not liquid propane).

    Let's say you fill your one-pounder FULL (leaving no headspace) then leave it in the parking lot in the back of your SUV in the summer with the windows rolled up. The cylinder gets warm. The liquid expands. The cylinder vents some propane through its safety relief valve but then ruptures if the valve is not up to the task. Tell me it ain't never gonna happen.

- 'TS' commented:

  The "chillin'" method is what was recommended by the manufacturer of the filling device that I bought from Cabela's MANY years ago. It works well. I don't put mine in the freezer, I just sink them in an ice chest full of ice for about 15 minutes before filling.

- Ron Brown:

  Regardless of your refill method, it is most important that you check, with a scale, the weight of your one-pounder after refilling. Otherwise, you are just guessing. I hate to be hardnosed about this, but propane is not something to estimate or guesstimate. I've come to have a very healthy respect for the stuff.

  Just because you've done it for years without checking on a scale and without incident is not proof of its safety. After all, you might cross the road without looking for years. And get away with it for years. But that doesn't mean it's safe to do so.

  I use an inexpensive plastic scale (Salter brand) with a 0-7 lb. weight range capability. As mentioned above (i.e. in Part 3 of Propane for Preppers), anything above 865 grams or 30.5 ounces gross weight indicates overfilling. The excess needs to be bled off. If you've been estimating all along, please buy a scale and check out your actual results. You might be surprised.

  This really is important.

- **Comment #4.** 'TPS' commented :

  Outstanding article! One of the BEST, I've ever read or seen on any preparedness website. Well Done! (and thank you!!)

- **Comment #5.** 'M' commented:

  Interesting read for sure, thank you Ron, I really enjoyed it!

  However.....

  As you said: "On the other hand, if you are not mechanically inclined and do not have an outside area in which to work, refilling-one pound propane tanks may not be for you."

  This should cover 80% of the population.

  I'm easily capable of refilling the cylinders, but why?

  A new one pounder from Wally is $2.97. If as you said you save $1.97, there is a difference of One dollar. To save the one dollar, you need to buy an adapter (Sears $ 8.95) a cap and O-ring if there is a leak (about $3.65), and a scale to check proper fill. And of course there is a question how much your time is worth.

  So in recap: 80% of the population should not try this, and for the other 20% this is not a saving.

  It is still a fun read!

  - Ron Brown:

    Thanks for your input, Magyar, but your 80% figure should, in my mind, be more like 10%. For example, I know a lady who was brought up in a house full of servants. She literally had never changed a light bulb before she was married. She laughs about it today, telling how she sat on the bed and cried when her new husband forced her to do it. In my mind, SHE is the kind of person who has no business refilling propane one-pounders.

    And I agree, the cost savings are small. TODAY. But there's comfort in knowing how to do things. I no longer change the oil in my car, for example. But I've done it and I know how. And if you take that little capability and multiply it by a hundred – or a thousand – other things that you know how to do, it gives you some independence. When TSHTF, I would prefer to feel I can cope as opposed to feeling helpless.

Being able to refill a propane one-pounder could, in the right circumstance, be priceless knowledge. I have a book out on Amazon ("The New 2000-Hour Flashlight") where one reader commented, "I live in South Florida and wish I had had this information when after Hurricane Wilma we were 3 weeks without electricity." THAT is when you need to know how to refill propane one-pounders. TODAY, I agree, saving $1.97 is a "who cares?" But THEN, it means you'll have light; it means you'll be able to cook supper. I guess maybe it's a prepper thing

- **Comment #8.** 'M' commented:
I have Worhtington brand 1 pounders and no where on them does it say anything about "Never refill this cylinder."

  - Ron Brown on March 12, 2015 at 7:40 pm said:
  Thanks for your interest, M, and for your time to write up your remarks. In fact, I have a Worthington one-pounder setting on the desk beside me as I write this. Under HANDLING AND STORAGE the label says "4. Never refill this cylinder." If your Worthington cylinders do not say that, then it is most likely that you are looking at older cylinders. You yourself may have owned them for several years OR they may have been setting on a store shelf for several years. To the folks who rebuild antique cars, this would be called "new-old stock." Picture a car headlight, brand new, still sealed in the factory box. But manufactured in 1921. Mom-and-pop hardware stores are full of new-old stock. Propane one-pounders are no exception. I assure you that

Worthington one-pounders made and sold TODAY are labeled, "Never refill this cylinder."

- **Comment #11.** 'D' commented:
  Electric fences were not around in Mark Twain's day. The quote came from Will Rogers.

  "There are three kinds of men: The ones that learns by reading. The few who learn by observation. The rest of them have to pee on the electric fence for themselves." ~ Will Rogers

- Ron Brown:
  My bad.

PART FOUR

PROPANE FOR PREPPERS

Part Four

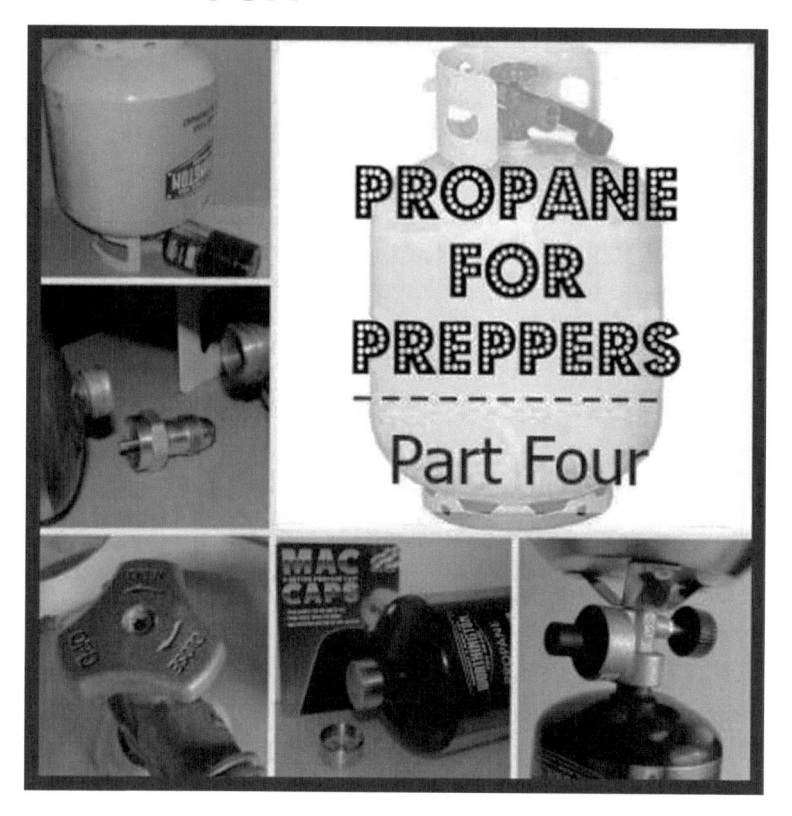

Refilling a 20-Pounder

At issue is the refilling of a 20-pounder (BBQ-tank size) from the big supply-tank that feeds your home. Several big-tank sizes exist. For discussion purposes, let's refer to the big supply-tank (whatever its size) as the 'nurse-tank.'

First, we have legalities to ponder. Are there any federal regulations (EPA, DOT, DOE, etc.)? How about the state? County? Township? City? Zoning laws?

Maybe life would be simpler if I just became a certified propane serviceman. But where do I get the training? I'm not even sure what to Google for.

And let's not forget the gas supplier. We own the gas but he owns the tank. Can we legally disconnect from his tank and then use his tank to fill smaller tanks? 'Cause if his tank gets damaged . . .

I feel a copout coming over me.

Tell you what. I'll share the little bit I know about the mechanical process of transferring propane from one tank to another but you're on your own regarding legal requirements. Fair enough? Just remember, ignorance of the law is no excuse. So here we go . . .

There are two refill methods, (1) liquid-transfer and (2) gas-transfer.

Liquid-transfer. Your big nurse-tank has a pipe inside that goes from top to bottom (like the tube inside a pressurized aerosol spray can). As the tank comes to you, the top of the pipe is capped off (but it is possible to install a hand valve at the top of that pipe). The gas company installs such a valve and uses this top-to-bottom pipe to pump the gas out of your tank if the tank is moved (should you cancel them as a supplier, for example).

If you remember, when refilling a one-pounder we had to turn the supply-tank upside down to get liquid propane to exit the valve. But here we have a pipe that goes to the bottom of the tank where the liquid lives plus a (potential) valve at the top of the tank. The top of our nurse-tank could thus host two valves – a 'gas-valve' to feed the house with gaseous propane plus a 'liquid-valve' for use in refilling smaller tanks.

To refill a 20-pounder via liquid-transfer we need to have the correct valve installed on the top-to-bottom pipe plus a high-pressure hose with the appropriate fittings on each end (to reach from the nurse-tank to the 20-lb. receiving-tank). We'd connect the two tanks with the hose, open both valves, and let the games commence. You can hear when the transfer stops. OPD would prevent us from overfilling.

(Where do you obtain the valves and hoses? Your gas company already has, for its own use, everything you need. All you have to do is convince them to sell you the stuff.)

After refilling, we'd check the weight of the 20-lb. receiving-tank. The total weight should not exceed the tare weight of the receiving-tank (as stamped on its collar) plus the 20 lbs. net of propane we just transferred. Conversely, should the 20-lb. receiving-tank be underfilled, we could chill the receiving tank and take additional propane on board.

Gas-transfer. We can also use the gas line (that goes to our house) rather than the liquid line. Note that the 'gas-transfer' method is much slower. It will take 30-90 minutes or more to fill a 20-pounder.

As before, when connecting the big supply-tank to the small receiving-tank, we need a high-pressure propane hose with appropriate fittings on each end. We would (1) turn off the nurse-tank that feeds the house. Then (2) disconnect the supply-line that runs from the valve to the house. Note that any household appliance with a pilot light would have to be relit afterwards (plus there might be air in the lines).

(3) We'd connect our high-pressure hose between the nurse-tank gas-valve and the 20-lb. receiving-tank. Then we'd (4) open the valve on each end and let the games begin.

(5) We would have to keep the receiving-tank colder than the supply-tank throughout (to lower its pressure and condense the entering gas). One way to do this would be to set the 20-pounder in a tub of ice water. Another way would be to trickle water from a garden hose over the receiving-tank for the duration. As with the liquid-transfer method, OPD would prevent us from overfilling.

So, in round numbers, those are the basics. You can find YouTube videos demonstrating both methods. Please note that the safety precautions taken by the makers of these videos are not always the greatest. (What part of 'understatement' don't you understand?)

If you do attempt refilling a 20-pounder, leather gloves and safety goggles are appropriate. No smoking. No sparks. And if something goes wrong, it will not blow up your garage. It will blow up your neighborhood. Well, that's an exaggeration. Explosions are rare. It will only burn down your neighborhood. But if you aspire to be stage-center on the 6:00 o'clock news, this could be your debut. As an added bonus you'll receive an official letter on company stationery from your fire insurance agent (suitable for framing).

Come to think of it, maybe you should talk to your fire insurance agent first, before attempting to refill a twenty-pounder. Ya think?

Storage of One-Pounders

Storage is a troublesome topic for me. I've come to have a lot of respect for propane (a.k.a. fear). I don't want to store the cylinders in my living quarters. Ditto for my basement workshop.

Why? Because they might leak. That's one reason. But if I ever have a fire, a few propane cylinders venting into the flames at random intervals (if not exploding) will not make things better. That's the real reason. I don't want the firemen sitting in the truck waiting for the show to be over before combatting my house fire.

My garage, attached to the house, poses the same problem. And my outdoor sheds/barns get hot in the summer. I'm sure they go over 120° F with no-one being aware of it. And it's humid from time to time. Which contributes to rusting.

Here's my experience. A year after formal retirement I received job offer in Canada. So we left our house as-is (unoccupied but fully furnished) and rented an apartment near the job.

Before departing for Canada, I took all the combustible items I could find – gas cans, kerosene, paint thinner, charcoal lighter fluid, half a dozen propane cylinders, etc. – and locked them up in a metal shed a hundred feet away from the house.

The shed and everything in it was largely ignored for the two years I was gone. When I returned, the propane one-pounders had all rusted (as shown in the photo below).

Okay. So I can't store the cylinders in my living quarters. Or basement. Or garage. Or in a non-air-conditioned shed or barn. How am I supposed to store these things?

I've read, incidentally, that you should remove the paper labels from propane cylinders so that moisture doesn't get trapped under the label where it will contribute to rusting. That advice turns out to be armchair science. I did not remove the labels and all six of my one-pounders looked like the photo below. All of the rust was on the shoulders of the cylinders; none of the rust was under the labels. Translation: The theory is wrong; the advice is bogus.

Anyway, presented below is my storage solution. It's what I came up with. Is it any good? Don't know. Will it work? Don't know. Come back in ten years and ask me. Note that I did not use any mastic when sealing the storage containers. I want to be able to open them, and do it easily, at least once a year for our family camping trip.

I have a fair supply of empty 5-gallon plastic pails with tops. They originally contained driveway sealer. They seem to make excellent storage containers for one-pounders.

There is enough room to stand four one-pounders on the floor of a 5-gallon pail. Plus you can squeeze in a Bernzomatic-type soldering cylinder should you happen to have one. There's enough additional space for two more one-pounders to be laid crossways on top of the upright, bottom cylinders. (To avoid things clanging around, I wrap the two horizontal cylinders in bubblewrap.) So a 5-gallon pail will hold a total of six one-pounders plus a soldering cylinder.

I also add a desiccant to absorb any air-borne moisture inside the 5-gallon pail. If there is no moisture in the air, then the metal cylinders cannot rust, eh? I use calcium chloride. To hold the desiccant I punch holes in the lid of a half-pint canning jar (which then resembles a salt shaker) and stretch a piece of cloth over the mouth of the jelly jar (but under the lid) so that no calcium chloride pellets leak out through the punched holes. I am at pains to prevent the calcium chloride (sold as driveway de-icer in the winter) from touching the steel propane cylinders. Calcium chloride – $CaCl_2$ – is corrosive to steel.

A desiccant expands as it absorbs moisture. So each of my desiccant jars is only half-full of calcium chloride. I put two such jars in each 5-gallon pail. I slide the jars between the standing cylinders so that they (the desiccant jars) are upright, vertical.

Lastly, I seal the lid of the 5-gallon pail with duct tape. I put three continuous windings around the lid, making the first wrap flush with the top edge of the lid itself and spiraling successive wraps (generously overlapped) downwards onto the body of the pail.

One of the dangers in storing propane is that, if a cylinder gets hot (in the 120-130° F range or higher), the cylinder's safety valve can spurt out a bit of propane to relieve the pressure. With propane, temperature and pressure are directly related.

This is especially dangerous in a confined space (the hull of a boat, for example). Repeated ventings (that no-one is even aware took place) from a bunch of stored propane cylinders can be disastrous.

Personally, I don't want the cylinders in my 5-gallon pail to get hot and vent propane into the bucket. If I lived in Texas or Florida where summer temperatures reach absurd levels this would be an even greater concern.

Let me share an experience that might reveal how we can help ourselves temperature-wise.

It was winter. I lived in a rented house. Times were tough. I got permission from the landlord to install a homemade barrel stove (in which to burn wood for heat). The stove worked fine but it was positioned less than six inches away from an exterior wall. The inside surface of the wall was wood paneling. And the wall got hot. Very hot. As in, "Ouch! That's hot!"

After a few days of worry, I Scotch-taped aluminum foil to the wall behind the stove. At which point you could lay your hand flat on the wall and the wall was cold. Icy cold. As in, "Wow! That's amazing!"

So we could wrap our plastic pail in aluminum foil. That would be one way to help with the temperature problem. But foil is fragile, easily torn.

As an alternative we could spray-paint our pail with aluminum paint. Or white paint. And wrap it in bubblewrap. Or wrap it in a bat of fiberglass insulation. Or stand it in a cardboard box filled with sawdust. Or do all of the above and then bury it in the cool earth. In the shade. These are all just suggestions on how to cope with the temperature question.

Carbon Monoxide

The label on Coleman one-pounders contains a surprisingly prominent warning about carbon monoxide (CO). No other brand even mentions carbon monoxide. Older Coleman labels don't mention carbon monoxide. Coleman one-pounders sold in Canada don't mention carbon monoxide.

So what gives? Was (or is) the Coleman warning part of some legal settlement? That's all I can think of.

Things that smolder (cigarettes, charcoal briquettes, incense) give off large quantities of carbon monoxide. That's why it's not safe to use a charcoal grill inside the house. Things that burn with a clear flame (stove burners, lanterns) give off miniscule (tiny, tiny) quantities of carbon monoxide.

A few years ago, in researching *Lanterns, Lamps, and Candles: A User's Guide*, I tested all sorts of lamps and lanterns (one at a time) in a room with a CO detector. The detector, factory-preset to 30 ppm (parts per million), never went off. I began to doubt it was even working until I moved a stick of burning incense nearby. Then it screamed.

But where should I position the detector? Above or below the lamp being tested? Is CO heavier than air?

That seemed like a straightforward question. But when I Googled it, some answers said CO is lighter than air and rises; some said it's heavier and pools in the basement; some said it's about the same and rises because it's mixed with the hot exhaust of the burning lamp. Good grief.

I could not find authoritative answers to my questions so I finally shelled out a hundred bucks for a meter and did my own testing.

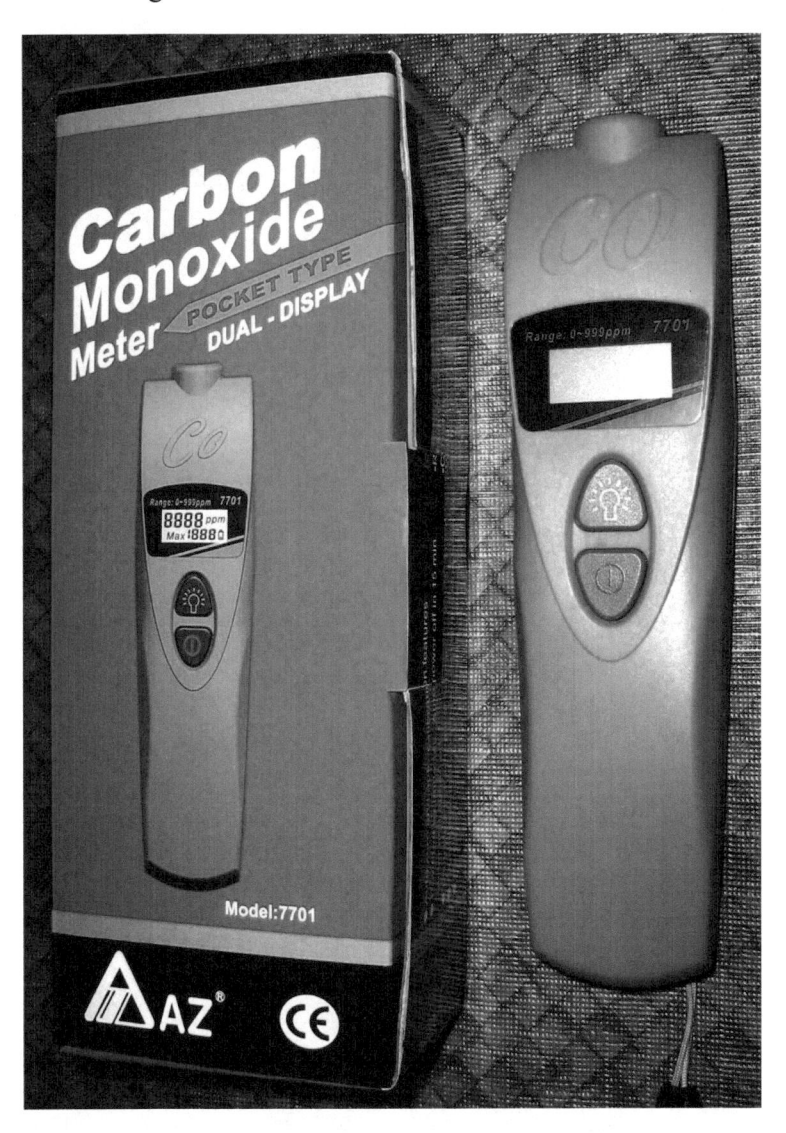

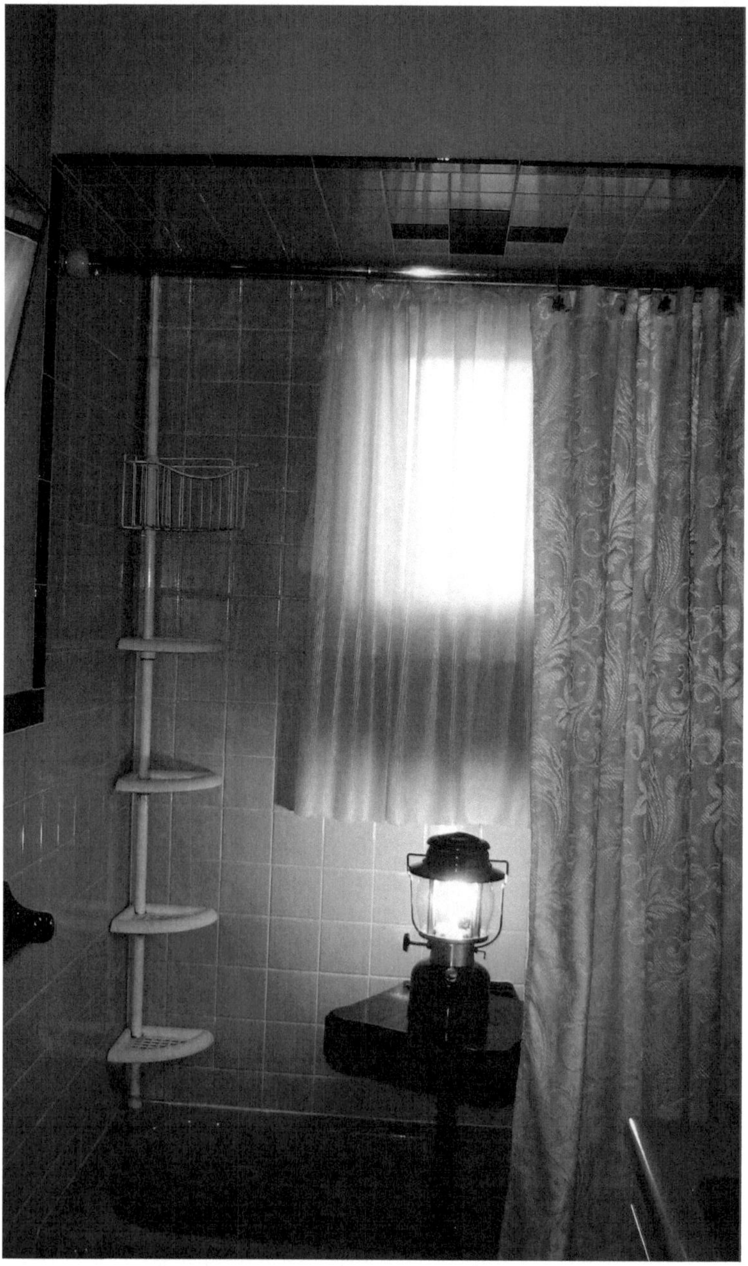

Carbon monoxide proved to be elusive stuff. Even in a closed shower stall it was hard to get a reading. The meter measured in 1 ppm increments and had a measuring range from zero to 999 ppm. Out in general living quarters it was virtually impossible to get a reading.

I found that wick-type kerosene lamps (that generate light from a simple burning flame) produce more CO than do pressure lanterns that employ a mantle. After burning for one hour in a closed shower stall, for example, my average meter-reading for a Rayo wick-type kerosene lamp was 20 ppm.

For a propane mantle-lamp, the average reading was only 5 ppm. (And this, remember, is after one hour of burning inside a closed shower stall with no ventilation of any kind in the bathroom – no fan, window closed, bathroom door closed.)

One ppm is not very big. A carton of paint at the hardware store holds four one-gallon cans. Visualize, if you will, 17 gallons of paint – a stack of boxes, four high, plus one extra gallon on top. A single drop of paint thinner, measured with an eye-dropper and spread evenly across all 17 gallons, constitutes one part per million.

Oxygen Starvation

Everything that burns consumes oxygen – your fireplace, your gas range in the kitchen, the candles on your birthday cake. When your house is crowded with people, each breathing and consuming their own bit of oxygen, the available supply goes down even faster.

The fix is easy. Open a window. Let in some fresh air.

But what if you don't? What are the symptoms of oxygen starvation and what are the consequences if you ignore it?

The symptoms are these. Early on, you may report 'feeling just fine' even though you are pale and confused. Later, you have no energy/strength/stamina. You have shortness of breath, chest tightness, blue coloring around your lips, tingling fingers, increased pulse, you want to sleep.

Oxygen starvation can also occur at high altitudes (where the air is 'thin') and when breathing mixtures of gases with low oxygen content (diving, for example).

If you're living at a high altitude, say, and ignore the symptoms, the long-term consequences can be extreme fatigue, waking at night gasping for breath, loss of eyesight, loss of short term memory, and progressive weakening of the heart muscle leading to heart failure.

But that's the long-term extreme. As far as unvented propane appliances are concerned (your kitchen stove, for example), the fix is easy. Open a window. Let in some fresh air.

Selected Reader Comments, Part Four

- **Comment #1.** 'D' commented:
  I have stored for years the 1 pound cylinders in a 4" piece of PVC pipe and have not had any problems at all. I capped and glued one end of the pipe and put a screw type clean out cap on the other end for removal purposes. You can even bury them if you first put some pipe putty on the threaded end before screwing it closed.
  - Ron Brown:
    Thanks D. I'll have to try that. If I may ask, what results do you get? What's the longest you've stored a cylinder (months? years?) and what shape was it in

when you took it out of storage? Any rust or corrosion? How much does it cost? Sounds like maybe the pipe, end cap, glue, and screw-type clean-out cap might cost more than the one-pounder itself. But it sure would be nice to safely store a couple of one-pounders from one camping trip to the next.....

- 'D' responded:
  I don't remember the actual cost because it was a long time ago. I went to Lowes and bought everything I needed. I cut the 10' piece of 4" pipe in half and I am able to store five cylinders in each section. I have had some of them stored for about four years and they still look brand new, even the ones I have buried look new, I dug them up after about a year to check on them and can't tell any difference between the ones kept indoors.

- Ron Brown:
  Great! Thanks for sharing. As I said in the article, storage of one-pounders is a troublesome topic for me. Your first-hand, hands-on info is the very best kind.

- **Comment #5.** 'G' commented:
Very interesting and informative series. Couple questions for Ron...So from what I took away from your posts, I am better off getting my 20# tanks refilled at the local mill or Tractor Supply as opposed to doing the exchange, as I will actually be getting what I pay for? And DH (who has some more experience with this than me) has mentioned needing to 'burp' the tank before refilling...with all the safety features in the newer tanks, I'm thinking this is safer than it used to be, and may result in a fuller tank? We use natural gas/electric to power our home, but we are campers and regularly use the one pounders and 20#ers...learning to refill the one

pounders for use with the appliances we have from a 20# is useful information, I will be printing off all of this series. Thank you!

- Ron Brown:
Thanks for your interest. Are you better off getting your tanks refilled at the local mill as opposed to the exchange? Probably. Blue Rhino (for example) only puts in 15 lbs. of propane whereas your local mill stops filling at 20. But some dealers charge by the pound and others charge a flat fee to top off the tank. So it's really a case-by-case problem. You'd need to weigh the tank before after filling and see how much you got versus the price paid. It's a nuisance but not rocket science. Most times, dollar-wise, you're better off going to the mill. The exchange is more convenient but you pay for the convenience.

Not sure what "burping" is. If you open the one of the new OPD (Overfill Protection Device) tanks without any appliance being attached, no propane comes out (by design). Will burping (whatever it is) result in a fuller tank? I hope not. You MUST leave some headspace. Don't put in more than 20 lbs., even if you can.

- **Comment #7.** 'B' commented:
I am wondering why you only use propane? Coleman fuel/white gas uses 1 gallon to 5-1 lb tanks. The fuel, if left sealed, can easily last 20+ years. If smaller amounts of fuel are wanted they make 1 quart plastic bottles. If necessary the Coleman fueled equipment can run on regular unleaded gasoline. 1 lantern can run for 12+ hours on high without a refill. The stoves are just as nice and boil water faster. Just seems easier to bring 1 backpack stove and 1 small lantern and 1 gallon of fuel and have it last 2+ weeks of use instead of hauling around 5 tanks as

back ups and 2 on the equipment for a total of 2-1 lb tanks.

So a 5 gallon gas can of white gas (filled in Amish country for less than $20) would equal to about 25-1 lb cylinders. See the space savings too!

- 'B' added:

  Sorry I meant 7-1lb tanks.

  - Ron Brown:

    Hi B. I do not "only use propane." I have a YouTube video, for example, explaining how to convert a gas pressure lantern (that is, Coleman fuel) to kerosene. And I personally have lanterns that run on Coleman fuel and propane and kerosene and diesel and alcohol. I don't belong to a propane religion or a Coleman-fuel religion. When TSHTF, whatever fuel is available, I want a lantern that will run on it. When it comes to prepping and survival, redundancy is the name of the game.

- **Comment #8.** 'EP' commented:

  I am a certified propane gas service tech and trainer. I recover gas from the larger storage tanks you refer too here and I would like to come on your article from two perspectives

  first   safty

  there is, a reason we put the label on the liquid withdrawal valve on those thanks. You can and I have been severely burned from the liquid gas (-44 deg) also if you just take the cap off and the spring 9n the excess flow valve in side the liquid withdrawal valve is bad (more times than good) then you will have an explosive release of liquid gas and a vapor cloud that could blow,up an entire block. Second legal issues. Unless you purchased the tank it is the property of the propane company and tampering with any part of the tank could land you in hot water and if injury occurs because of your tampering with the tank you are liable for any and all damage or loss of life or injury just like the propane company.

This is exactly why your articles are putting people at sever risk of legal actions and possibly death of themselves or their families and loved ones and entire neighborhoods.

I have had to have whole subdivisions evacuated because of a gas leak.

I seriously would reevaluate your legal responsibility by posting these tips that are both legally wrong and pose a possible serious safty risk. Are you willing to take a law suit because you gave people a drop of information that in reality takes a minimum of 2 years to become certified in. I would reassess these "helpful tips"

- **Comment #9.** 'A' commented:
  I'd like to point out that CO is lighter than air and so will accumulate from the top of an enclosed space downwards.

  CO has a mass of $12+16=28$ g/mol, while the mean mass of air is 28.8 g/mol

  Additionally, the CO is generated during combustion, and is therefore likely to be warmer than the air in the room.

  CO_2, on the other hand, should accumulate from the floor upwards, once it has cooled, since its mass is 44 g/mol.

  - Ron Brown:
    Thank you, A. That is information I looked for and could not locate online. And it confirms my personal experience: carbon monoxide readings at the ceiling, nothing at floor level. Thanks again.

PART FIVE

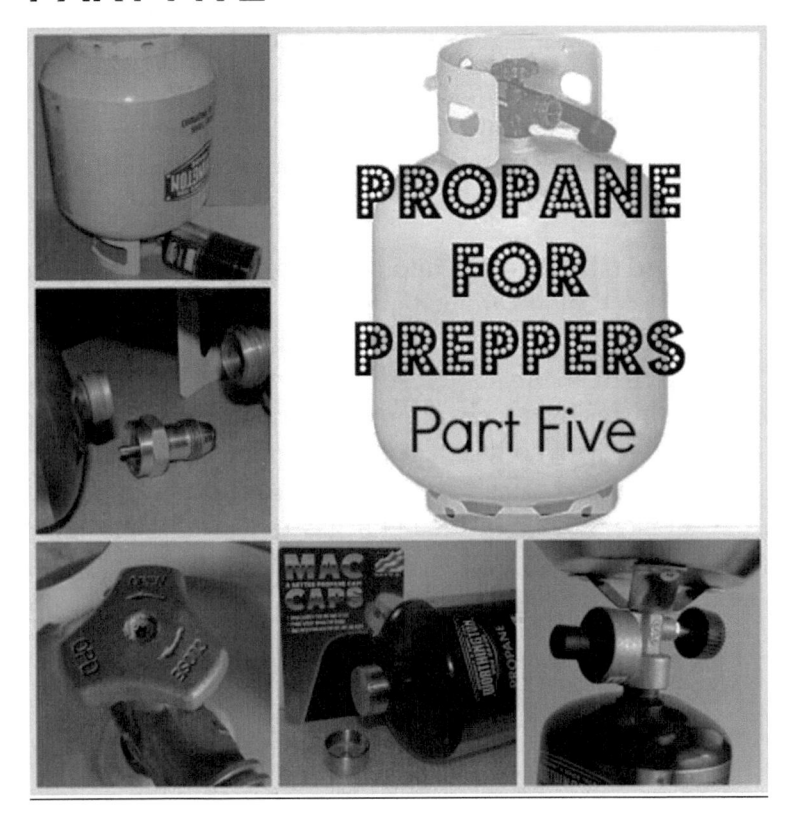

Carbon Monoxide Revisited

Today, December 17, 2014, our series on propane comes to an end. In this installment I'm going to reopen the topic of carbon monoxide. Gaye Levy forwarded a letter to me that reveals just how troublesome and conflicted (not to mention huge) this topic is. After seeing the letter, I realized my time would be better spent addressing this concern than any other.

Here's the letter:

"I started reading up about propane stove/burners and carbon monoxide. There's a ton of conflicting advise on the internet about those two. Even the Mr. Buddy Heater threads have some people who argue about how best to use it and where not to. For instance, some people say they are meant for indoor construction sites, not for enclosed rooms.

"I used one years ago during a power outage. The room was 12x12 and adjoined a 12 x 10 room and a 10 x 10 room, I still got a bit of a headache from it. I think it was on that thread I read someone say not to use a natural gas oven to heat a room. I used one once for that purpose. Had no ill effects. I went on to read how some Yahoo asked what's the difference between a propane camping stove and a natural gas oven, imho he never got a clear answer. Someone replied that the natural gas ovens are vented as being the difference, which is clearly false, at least the several natural gas ovens I've used didn't have Any kind of venting.

"I read on a tiny house blog where some people say don't worry about using propane stove/burners in enclosed spaces, one guy mentioned how millions of people in Asia use propane everyday with no ill effects. Older people chime in and say how they used them in the old days in the unitedstate, in contrast to those who freak out about the very idea of using a propane device inside.Then there's the fellas using the Coleman dual fuel camping stoves in the back of a camper or in a tiny house with no ill effects. While other guys insist on running a hose through the wall to an outside tank for their propane stoves, and yet still more guys just run a hose under the kitchen sink to their 20lb. tank.

"The beer brewing guys talk about the subject quite a bit. Seems a lot of them use turkey fryers in their garages and some of them would prefer to brew in the basement during the Winter. They ask themselves: will propane work?

"I came across an imported wok propane burner, it could get to 100,000 BTU. Pretty impressive, but way too hot for my needs.

"I looked at the RV drop-in and slide-in propane stove top burners. On the BTU side, they seemed to all run a little low. Campers they are used in - are enclosed - yet, I didn't read about anyone freaking out about the use of them. I'm considering building a wooden box one can drop or slide into so I can use it on the kitchen counter top.

"I found a propane single burner on Amazon which was listed as safe for indoor use. In the Q&A section it appeared the manufacturer was saying the reason they are safe for indoor use is that they are small and only give off a small amount of carbon monoxide. ...Then I read elsewhere how some people say the only real danger from using a Coleman propane camping stove inside is from using it too long, from trying to heat a room or house, and from leaving it unattended. I get the idea it's ok to use one if a window is open a crack. (In contrast, one guy on the beer brewing thread said he kept a garage door open two feet - and a backdoor open - and still got high carbon monoxide readings on his detector inside his house after using his propane turkey fryer) On the Coleman website, in the description of some of the propane camping stoves, it says, use during emergencies. I'm guessing this is their way of saying they're not going to say it's safe to use indoors, but you might be just fine.? The rest of the stoves simply state something like, "for outdoor use only". I wonder if there's a difference between the two groups or if it's just worded differently?

"This subject would make a good follow up to the propane series. (Hint. Hint.)

"I also came across a company which sells (imported from India) small kerosene single burner stoves, they looked like they might be worthwhile. However; the importer does caution that they come from a third world country and might be a bit banged up, dinged, scratched or have a bit of rust. Millions(?) of people use them with great success though.

"I need to read some more. Pardon me if that was a bit long winded and sloppy, the subject matter is rather wide."

It is, indeed, a wide-ranging topic. Please be advised that, in reopening the carbon monoxide discussion (just a bit further on), I must repeat some of what was presented in Propane for Preppers, Part Four.

*****

Philosophy. Whatever I say, some people will agree with me, some will disagree, and some will be confused. And feelings will run high. So let me first present a bit of 'philosophy' (for lack of a better term).

Rationalizing is "the attempt to explain or justify one's behavior or attitude with logical, plausible reasons, even when those reasons are not true or appropriate."

People can rationalize just about anything. Consider a 'discussion' I had with my brother-in-law. We'd been talking awhile and at one point he commented, "Aw, that's just conspiracy theory. I don't believe any conspiracy theories."

In the interest of reasonableness, I said, "Sam, we all participate in conspiracies. How about Santa Claus? All adults conspire about Santa. We all lie to our children . . ."

He interrupted. "Santa Clause is REAL. Santa Claus is the spirit . . ."

"No, Sam! I'm not talking about the 'spirit of giving.' I'm saying there is no fat man dressed in a red outfit trimmed in fur that lives at the North Pole . . ."

My sister rose to her husband's defense. "How do YOU know? How do you know there isn't a fat man in a red suit living at the North Pole? Can you prove to me there isn't?"

OMG.

The point to this little narrative is that human beings can rationalize just about anything. War, torture, propane safety, Santa Claus, anything.

*****

Continuing for a moment with the philosophy bit, we all seek perfection but perfection does not exist on this earth, in this realm.

I can give you (what I think) is good advice about marriage. Raising children. Driving a car. Running a factory. It will be good advice but not perfect. There are no absolutes.

Ditto for propane safety. Ditto for carbon monoxide.

Stupid stuff happens in committee meetings. That means stupid stuff sometimes appears on product labels. And stupid stuff sometimes appears in government regulations. Do you think the Coleman Company, when speaking in public on matters of safety and carbon monoxide, is divinely withheld from error? How about OSHA?

You can rationalize it however you want.

What Are the Risks Surrounding Propane?

- Inhaling propane vapors

- Oxygen depletion

- Inhaling products of combustion (carbon monoxide)

- Fire and explosion

- Frostbite from a cylinder leaking liquid propane

Frostbite was covered in the 3rd installment of 'Propane for Preppers' where we described the refilling of one-pounders. The other four items are discussed below.

Inhaling Propane Vapors

A little puff of gas always escapes when you turn on the kitchen stove burner. Sometimes you can even smell it. The same thing happens when connecting or disconnecting a one-pounder to a camp stove or lantern. Inhaling some of it is virtually unavoidable. The question is, how much harm does it do you?

In answer, propane, although non-toxic, is an asphyxiate gas meaning it can replace oxygen and suffocate you. Teenagers have been known to inhale propane in an attempt to get high. They put a plastic bag over a BBQ tank, fill the bag with propane, then inhale from the bag. Unfortunately, when their lungs are full of propane, oxygen is blocked from entering the lungs.

Here's the tricky part. Our urge to breathe is triggered by a high level of carbon dioxide in the air. Our body knows that if carbon dioxide is high then oxygen must be low. And so our body tells us that it's time to breathe. However, propane displaces the carbon dioxide in our lungs right along with the oxygen; a high level of carbon dioxide never exists. So our body never gets the signal to breathe. What was that 911 number again?

Propane is heavier than air and pools in the bottom of your lungs (blocking oxygen absorption into your bloodstream). The burner on your kitchen stove is lower than your face so you inhale a minimal amount. When you attach/detach one-pounders from your camp stove or soldering torch you can position the fittings (and any escaping gas) lower than your face. You can also hold your breath for a moment to avoid inhaling propane. You can also (it seems to me; I've never read this anywhere) stand on your head and take a few deep breaths. The same gravity that deposited propane in the bottom of your lungs should remove it, no?

Oxygen Starvation

The burners on your kitchen gas stove consume oxygen. So does the oven. So does your wood stove. So does your lantern – whether it burns kerosene or propane or Coleman fuel.

Your wood stove has a chimney and is thus 'vented.' Venting gets rid of unwanted products of combustion. Your gas range in the kitchen (typically four burners plus an oven) is not vented. But whether an appliance is vented or not, the oxygen it uses in the burning process comes from the inside air.

Outside air is 21% oxygen. Inside air is something below that. You, your wood stove, your birthday candles, your girlfriend, and the family dog all compete for the available oxygen. If the oxygen level is depleted too far you suffer 'oxygen starvation.'

You say you feel 'just fine' even though you are pale and confused. Later, you have no energy/strength/stamina. You have shortness of breath, chest tightness, blue coloring around your lips, tingling fingers, increased pulse, you want to sleep.

The fix is easy. Ditch the girlfriend. Well, okay. Open a window. Let in some fresh air.

Oxygen starvation (having nothing whatsoever to do with propane) can occur at high altitudes where the air is 'thin.' If you ignore the symptoms, long-term consequences in such an environment can be blindness and heart failure.

But that's the long-term extreme. As far as propane appliances are concerned (your kitchen stove, for example), the fix is easy. Open a window. Let in some fresh air.

Inhaling the Products of Combustion

As a youngster, I was repeatedly lectured on the dangers of carbon monoxide. Why? Because my mother had two schoolmates die from carbon monoxide poisoning. It made quite an impression on her tiny high school graduating class of twelve students.

The victims had been out 'parking' in a Model 'A' Ford. Heat for the Model A was pulled from the exhaust manifold. It was a poor design, well known for leaking exhaust gases. In this case it was fatal.

This, our fifth and last installment on propane, began with longish letter reflecting a lot of confusion and contradictory advice about carbon monoxide. I'm going to TRY and clear up some of the confusion. Wish me luck.

Carbon monoxide is produced when something burns with insufficient oxygen being present.

That seems simple enough but rapidly becomes confusing. Things that smolder when they burn (cigarettes, pipes, cigars, charcoal briquettes, incense) give off large amounts of carbon monoxide. If you want to test your carbon monoxide detector, bring a burning stick of incense nearby. The detector will SCREAM!

But why do these things smolder? After all, they have oxygen. They have access to the same air that we're breathing.

The answer is that they don't have ENOUGH oxygen. Each material has its own threshold of how much oxygen is required to burn with an open flame. Firewood will burn with the amount of oxygen found in the open air. Tobacco will not. Nor will steel.

An oxyacetylene cutting torch, for example, doesn't MELT a hole in steel. It BURNS a hole in steel. In a pure oxygen atmosphere, steel burns. Think about all the restrictions around medical patients who are on oxygen. Various materials will ignite and burn in a high-oxygen atmosphere that won't burn, or will only smolder, in our regular atmosphere.

So let me say it again. Carbon monoxide is produced when something burns with insufficient oxygen being present. That means insufficient oxygen for the material at hand, for the material that is burning.

There are three ways that a condition of 'insufficient oxygen' can come about.

(1) To burn with an open flame, the fuel in question (tobacco, for example) needs more oxygen than is present in ordinary air. We just covered that.

(2) The device (a stove burner, for example) can be out of adjustment; the fuel/air ratio can be incorrect. With propane, a 'lean' burn can be recognized when flames lift away from the burner and tend to go out. A 'rich' burn results in large flames, yellow in color. (Propane flames should be blue.) Both rich and lean burns reveal incomplete combustion and imply the production of carbon monoxide.

(3) In an enclosed area (room, cellar, garage, shed), combustion can deplete the available oxygen with the result that carbon monoxide (CO) is produced. It's produced as a byproduct of combustion rather than the normally-produced carbon dioxide (CO_2). Carbon dioxide is nontoxic and harmless to breathe.

Note that in this last scenario carbon monoxide can be produced even when the appliances are properly adjusted. When the oxygen is 'depleted' or partially used up it means there's not enough to go around. And in the combustion process it takes less oxygen to make CO (with one oxygen atom) than it does to make CO_2 (with two oxygen atoms).

So, in a situation with limited oxygen, CO is what gets made.

Carbon monoxide is colorless, odorless, and tasteless. That's what makes it so dangerous. It sneaks up on you.

Hemoglobin is the principle oxygen-carrying compound in your blood. Unfortunately, the attraction or affinity between CO and hemoglobin is many times stronger than the affinity between oxygen and hemoglobin so CO displaces the oxygen in your bloodstream. Your brain and heart do not get the oxygen that they need. You die.

Headache is the most common symptom of acute carbon monoxide poisoning. (Acute means 'brief and severe.') With oxygen depletion you are pale and confused; with carbon monoxide, you have a headache.

My experiments for measuring carbon monoxide were described in Part Four. I tested various lamps and lanterns, one at a time, inside a closed shower stall with no ventilation of any kind in the bathroom for one hour before measuring carbon monoxide. For a propane mantle lamp, the average reading was 5 ppm (parts per million).

There is always background carbon monoxide in the environment. That's why CO detectors for home use come from the store preset to 30 ppm. Any reading below '30' does not register; a reading below '30' is considered a nuisance value. And that's where propane mantle lamps register, down at the background-cum-nuisance level. (But that doesn't give you license to burn twenty of them in the same room.)

Product Warnings

Keep in mind the principles outlined above when reading the warnings on product labels. You'll find today's restrictions are more severe than the restrictions in years past. And safety restrictions in the USA are more severe than the restrictions in other countries.

Personally, I believe this results from lawsuits over the years and from companies trying to protect themselves with CYA (Cover Your Fanny) statements. They don't want to get hauled into court so, to preempt that possibility, they say 'never' do this and 'never' do that. With the blanket word 'never' they try and protect themselves from lawsuits. At least that's my opinion.

Here are a couple of examples.

Coleman one-pounders circa 1980 caution that "Refilling can be hazardous." Also, "Do not store . . . where temperatures exceed 130° F." Today, Coleman one-pounders say, "Never refill this cylinder. Refilling may cause explosion." Plus today's storage limit is set at 120° F.

So is it 120° or 130°? Is today's propane really different than yesterday's propane?

A 20-pound tank in the USA corresponds to a 9-kilogram tank in the metric world. (Nine kilograms equals 19.84 lbs.) In New Zealand, per their Environmental Protection Authority regulations: "The typical portable domestic LPG cylinder holds 9 kg. This is the largest cylinder you are allowed to have inside your home."

A Worthington (brand) 20-lb. tank in the USA is labeled thusly: "For outdoor use only. Do not use or store cylinder in a building, garage, or enclosed area."

Why are New Zealand tanks safer than American tanks?

Joking aside, to be absolutely honest, I can't rationalize this stuff.

Extinguishing a Propane Fire

The topic of propane fires is another toughy. If you Google for 'extinguishing a propane fire' the results are all over the map. At the top of the list will be directions for how to extinguish a fire on your propane BBQ grill. Unfortunately, a fire fueled by hamburger grease is confused with a fire fueled by propane.

On YouTube you'll see various groups of firemen practice turning off the propane valve on a large tank engulfed in flame. Five men hunker behind a 550-gallon-per-minute water spray, advance to the tank, shut off the valve, and retreat. The exercise is only worthwhile, of course, if the propane leak (the source of fuel for the flame) comes after the valve.

Explosions are rare but do happen. One classic incident was the 1998 Turkey Farm fire in Albert City, Iowa. An ATV (all-terrain vehicle) struck an above-ground pipe carrying propane. The pipe leaked. The propane caught on fire. The pipe was hooked to an 18,000 gallon tank. The firemen thought that if they stayed away from the ends of the tank they would out of the line of fire should the tank blow up.

They were wrong. The tank did blow up. Pieces of tank flew randomly in all directions. Two firemen were killed. Seven were injured.

Another famous case was in Ghent, West Virginia (2007). An old 500-gallon propane tank was being replaced with a new 500-gallon tank. A technician removed a plug that should not have been removed. It caused a leak. There was an explosion. Four people were killed. Six were injured.

These two examples notwithstanding, explosions are rare. And that fact is a testament to the propane industry.

Explosions are rare because every propane tank of every size, from one-pounders on up, have a pressure relief valve. In a fire, the tank heats, the pressure rises, the relief valve opens, propane exits the cylinder, is ignited, and forms a tower of flame like a fireworks fountain. It's visually impressive but very rarely does a tank go BOOM!

From what I've read, it is virtually impossible to extinguish a propane fire in a large tank. On small scale, the Coleman one-pounder label says: "IN CASE OF FIRE (1) Leave area quickly. Call for help. (2) Let cylinder burn out."

Translation: Evacuate the area. Call Ghost Busters. Don't mess with it yourself. Let the pros take over.

The Rest of the Story

Went to a lawn party. 15-year-old came around asking for a lighter. He'd been assigned the task of grilling the hamburgers. Of course he'd never cooked hamburgers before in his life. And never lit a gas grill for that matter. I offered matches. "No. I'll burn myself with those." As it turned out, nobody in the politically-correct group carried a cigarette lighter. So I followed him back to the grill with my matches.

He had turned the gas on before he went looking for a lighter. I could hear the hiss of escaping gas as well as smell something. Sauerkraut? After pondering the choices I decided that propane was the more likely candidate. I had him turn off the gas. We fanned the area as best we could to dissipate the gas that had already escaped. I lit a match and held it near the burner. He turned on the gas. Poof! He jumped. It singed the hair off the back of my knuckles.

"Well," I told him, "poof is better than whump! That's when you lose your eyebrows." He didn't smile.

I explained that you should light the match first and then turn the gas on. If it blows the match out (because of air in the line), turn the gas off and light a second match. Don't turn the gas on first and then fumble around looking for matches. That's the wrong way 'round. That's where poof and whump and KA-BOOM originate.

He didn't smile. He didn't speak. He didn't have to. The body language he'd been practicing for all of his fifteen years made his message abundantly clear. "Nobody's gonna tell me what to do."

His hostility was rewarded moments later with a dose of karma. Hamburger grease dripped into the grill . . . and the flames rose to his shoulders . . . and the smoke wafted across the yard and across the porch and into the house and set off the smoke detector . . . and there was much running to and fro.

And, yes, this is a true story. And I (for one of the few times in my own life) followed directions.

I evacuated the area. (I joined a bunch of people elsewhere in the yard.)

I called Ghost Busters (also known as the boy's parents).

I did not mess around with it myself. I let the pros handle it. And they did a great job. That's what parents are for. God bless 'em.

*****

Flashback. Remember my brother-in-law Sam from the beginning of this article? Turns out that when Sam was first married he lit a gas oven in the kitchen stove using a match. Like my 15-year-old friend in the story above, he turned on the gas before he went searching for matches. He found some. He struck one. The propane picked him up, carried him across the kitchen, and deposited him on the floor. His hair was gone so he got a wig in his Christmas stocking. I'm pretty sure it's where his adult belief in Santa Claus originated.

Dangers of Overfilling

A bit of 'fluid mechanics' here. If you step on your car's brake pedal, pressure is transferred via brake fluid (a liquid) to the car's wheels through small pipes (called brake lines). The brake system works because the brake fluid is not compressible. Liquids cannot be compressed.

If an air bubble gets trapped in a brake line, then your brakes feel spongy when you step on them. The air (a gas) is compressible. Gasses can be compressed. Pressure starts at the brake pedal but only makes it to the air bubble. Then it doesn't go any further until the air is sufficiently compressed.

When a liquid is heated, it expands. Picture a soda bottle filled to the brim with water. We put a cork in the bottle. The water in the bottle touches the bottom of the cork. There is no air, no 'headspace.'

We heat the bottle. Water is a liquid and does not compress. It expands. It pops the cork out of the bottle.

We repeat the experiment but this time we leave an inch of headspace between the top of the water and the bottom of the cork. We heat the bottle. The water expands. The headspace, the air, acts as a cushion. The air compresses. The cork stays.

If we provide too little headspace between the water and the cork, the expanding liquid will compress the air to the point there is enough pressure to pop the cork.

An LPG tank contains both liquid propane and gaseous propane. The propane is liquid only by merit of the fact that it is under intense pressure. If the liquid propane is heated, it expands. It behaves like any other liquid. It cannot be compressed.

If the propane tank is 100% full (zero headspace), it will burst if heated. If the tank has some headspace (but not enough), the liquid propane will expand as it is heated and the gaseous propane will compress. But at some point, if the pressure gets high enough, the tank will burst.

Propane tanks do have safety relief valves. But let's go back to our soda bottle. We have an empty plastic bottle. We punch a hole in its side. If we use our mouth to blow air into the bottle, the air escapes out the hole. If, however, we hook up the bottle to a big air compressor, our little hole is overwhelmed and the bottle bursts. The moral? If the pressure is high enough (from overheating), the propane tank's safety valve might be too small to prevent the tank from bursting.

Twenty-pound tanks (the size used on BBQ grills) are made to be refilled and have OPD (an Overfill Protection Device; a float inside the tank). Volume-wise, the tank could hold 25 lbs. of propane but OPD prevents it from being filled past 20 pounds (80%).

'One-pounders' for camping are not made to be refilled and, hence, have no OPD. The burden is on you to not fill them more than 80%.

You must leave some headspace. The last thing you need is an overfilled cylinder of propane to rupture in the middle of your camping gear, stashed in the back of your SUV on a stifling hot day in the office parking lot. If you live in a town like Phoenix or Dallas, where the metal buckle on your seatbelt gets hot enough to burn you, then you understand 'stifling hot.'

When propane exits a tank, the tank gets cold. If an appliance (camp stove, for example) calls for more gas than the one-pounder can accommodate, frost will build up on the outside of the cylinder. (The amount of fuel remaining in the cylinder is revealed by the frost line.)

When refilling, we want the supply tank to stay warm. But the act of emptying it has a cooling effect. Some people compensate for this cooling phenomenon by heating the supply tank. They set it out in the sun. Or out in the sun wrapped in black plastic. Or they soak it in hot water. This increases the pressure in the supply tank.

They also chill the receiving tank by putting it in the freezer. This reduces the pressure in the receiving tank. How long should you leave it in the freezer? On-line, I've seen everything recommended from "a few minutes" to overnight.

The MacCoupler (brand) refill adapter has an on-line video that demonstrates the refill procedure. THEIR procedure, let us be clear. They put the one-pounder, the receiving tank, in a freezer for half an hour before starting the refill. Frankly, I don't like that at all.

In refilling, propane moves from the supply-tank to the receiving-tank until the pressure equalizes between the two. But if you heat the supply tank and freeze the receiving tank it's oh-so-easy to overfill.

For example, I chilled a one-pounder in our home freezer for 45 minutes and set the 20-lb. supply tank out in the sun for the same period. 'Out in the sun' is an exaggeration. It was an overcast day, there was no direct sunshine, and the temperature was 70° F.

The tare weight of the one-pounder was 400 grams. After refilling, its gross weight was 1050 grams. The net weight of gas inside the one-pounder was thus 650 grams (1050 − 400 = 650). New, from the store, a one-pounder contains 465 grams. So I had overfilled my one-pounder by 40% (650 ÷ 465 = 1.40).

FYI, I burned off the excess gas with a camp stove. Fifty minutes of burn time on a one-burner stove (running full blast) brought the net weight of the receiving-tank down to 465 grams.

One way to NOT bleed off the overage is to install a soldering tip, set the propane cylinder outside, and turn on the soldering valve without lighting it (expecting the propane to leak away in the breeze). Without being lit, the cylinder will get cold, the tip will ice up, and little if any gas will escape. A curious phenomenon to say the least, but real. (And one we made good use of, if you remember, back in the refilling section.)

Purging

'Purging' is the act of flushing out the air inside a new (empty) tank and replacing it with propane. If the tank is not purged before its initial fill, the propane will be diluted with air and not up to the task of functioning as a fuel.

Purging is not a concern with one-pounders because they're already filled with propane when we bring them home from the store.

There are actually three materials to consider in the purging process: propane, air, and the water vapor in the air.

The wrong way to purge a tank is to use liquid propane. When the first bit of liquid propane rushes into the empty, virgin tank it evaporates and turns to a gas. To turn from liquid to gas requires heat. The heat is drawn from the sidewalls of the tank. Any water vapor in the air quickly coats the inside of the tank with ice. After the air is expelled, the ice remains. Which leaves you with water in your propane. In case you didn't already know it, water does not burn well when it reaches the flame in your appliance.

The new tank should therefore be purged or flushed out with *gaseous* propane. And it needs to be flushed out four times.

After the first flushing (accomplished by filling the receiving-tank to 15 psig with gaseous propane then exhausting the vapor to the atmosphere), the tank contains a 50/50 mix of air and propane.

After the second flushing, the tank contains 75% propane and 25% air.

After the third flushing, the tank contains 87.5% propane and 12.5% air.

After the fourth flushing, the tank contains 93.75% propane and 6.25% air.

And that's adequate. At that point the new tank can be disconnected from the gaseous-propane line, hooked up to a liquid-propane line, and filled.

Safety (and the double standard thereof)

If you compare the labels from propane cylinders old and new, you'll see the newer tanks are more restrictive. Why? Lawsuits over the years, I suspect, as well as companies playing CYA.

Coleman one-pounders circa 1980 caution that "Refilling can be hazardous." Also, "Do not store . . . where temperatures exceed 130° F."

Today, Coleman one-pounders say, "Never refill this cylinder. Refilling may cause explosion." Plus all of today's one-pounders (as well as soldering cylinders) set the storage limit at 120° F.

****

If you compare the rules in different countries, you'll see the USA is more restrictive. Probably, I suspect, for the same reasons (lawsuits and threats thereof).

A 20-pound tank in the USA corresponds to a 9-kilogram tank in the metric world. (Nine kilograms equals 19.84 lbs.) In New Zealand, per their Environmental Protection Authority regulations: "The typical portable domestic LPG cylinder holds 9 kg. This is the largest cylinder you are allowed to have inside your home."

A Worthington (brand) 20-lb. tank in the USA is labeled thusly: "For outdoor use only. Do not use or store cylinder in a building, garage, or enclosed area."

Which begs the question, why are New Zealand tanks so much safer than American tanks?

****

A 20-pounder has a brass needle valve. A one-pounder has a Schrader valve (with a rubber seat) like a bicycle tube. A 20-pounder is much more rugged and reliable than a one-pounder. And yet it is implicitly okay to store a one-pounder (a disposable, throw-away item) out in the woodshed with the camping gear whereas it is explicitly not okay for a 20-pounder. The 20-pounder is much safer setting outside in the rain, rusting.

****

In my kitchen, I have a four-burner (plus oven) kitchen range that runs on propane. It is not vented; that is, it has no chimney. We cook supper on it every night. And a lot happens on that stove during the home canning season as well as the week leading up to Thanksgiving.

I also have a two-burner stove for camping (Ozark Trail brand) that runs on propane. The owner's manual says, "WARNING For Your Safety: For Outdoors Use Only (outside any enclosure)."

Is it not odd that my unvented propane refrigerator is safe inside and my unvented propane soldering torch is safe inside and my unvented 4-burner propane kitchen range is safe inside but my 2-burner propane camp stove is not safe inside? The phrase 'double standard' keeps coming to mind.

****

How does Walmart do it? They have row upon row of flammable and combustible products – paint thinner, propane one-pounders, Coleman fuel – setting cheek to jowl on their shelves. And not just in the showroom. Palletloads in their warehouses and on their trucks. So does Home Depot and Lowe's and Sears and Target. And the guys who handle this stuff are not much smarter than me.

Remember Walmart's last propane fire? Neither do I.

Disposal of Empty Propane Cylinders

Unfortunately, I am completely stymied on the topic of cylinder disposal for one-pounders. I live in upstate New York (NOT the same as New York City). I Googled for 'NYS propane tank disposal.' Here are the first two results, top o' the list, one from Westchester County and the other from Huntington, Long Island:

http://environment.westchestergov.com/propane-tanks "To dispose of a one to two pound propane barbecue tank: Residual gas should be burned off through proper use of the grill. **Empty tanks may be disposed of in the garbage** or on bulk pick-up days. Never include a 1 or 2 pound barbecue tank with your glass, plastic or metal recyclables." [emphasis added]

http://www.huntingtonny.gov/content/13749/13849/17296/17306/17362/19899.aspx "Town of Huntington, Long Island, New York . . . The Recycling Center will accept, at no charge, propane tanks sized up to 25 lbs. . . . **Never put a propane tank out for trash collection with household garbage.**" [emphasis added]

I feel so much better now that the disposal issue has been clarified. Of course the labels on the cylinders themselves are helpful. "When empty discard in a safe place." Or "appropriate place."

Or maybe this one: "To discard, contact local refuse hauler or recycle center."

So I called my refuse hauler. I really did expect them to be knowledgeable. After all, they have a couple hundred garbage trucks on the road at any given time. Turned out they didn't have a clue. After a bit of phone-tag (and confirming I was talking about "the little green cylinders you hook up to camping lanterns") they told me to contact Home Depot or Lowe's and see what the people who sell these things suggest. You mean the clerk on duty in the sporting goods section of Walmart is the final authority on this stuff? Really?

I also chased down the number of the county recycling center. Got an automated recording who never called me back. (Imagine that.)

There's a principle in business management to the effect that, if management cannot decide something, then the decision, when push comes to shove, will be made at the lowest level in the organization (the machine operator typically). And the decision will be whatever is easiest for the guy making it.

So if the folks who make one-pounders cannot tell you how to dispose of the cylinder – nor can the vendor who sells it; nor can the trash collector; nor can the recycle center; nor can the internet; nor can the alphabet-soup government agencies – then the decision will be made by the customer. And it will be whatever is easiest for the customer. Right or wrong, empty one-pounders will go in the trash and get set out with the garbage. In my heart of hearts, I'm sure it happens hundreds if not thousands of times every day. Come on. Tell me it ain't never gonna happen.

Selected Reader Comments, Part Five

- **Comment #2.** 'OCB' commented:
  I have found your artical rather informative, all five, but for the generally public without any knowledge results could be devastating. NFPA [National Fire Protection Association], AGA [American Gas Association], and CGA [Compressed Gas Association] all aid in the safety of propane equipment, storage, transportation, sizing, and installation. I have spent 30 years in the HVAC field to include natural and propane work. Common scenes [sic] needs to prevail along with a working knowledge. The young tech was right. NFPA thing. Codes do change over time so was it required when new tank installed. Probably. Do we like to conform? Usually not. I like to think of it as a safety issue. Will concrete eventually corrode copper? Ever have a oil line in concrete leak? The old radiant copper systems are of ridged pipe and not soft tube. And yes I have seen concrete encased piping develops leaks. Nothing is really designed to last forever. In short when not familiar find some one who is. Safety first.

- Ron Brown:
  Thanks for your thoughtful response. To me the dilemma is whom to believe when the 'experts' disagree. I guess that's the crux of the matter. You say that you have seen concrete-encased piping develop leaks. No doubt you have. But was concrete-to-copper corrosion the problem? Or did a shady contractor bury some defective piping in the cement. 'Ah, it'll be years before it fails. And when it does we'll blame the concrete.' You say "the young tech was right . . . codes do change . . ." I challenge his 'rightness.' Is a new

code/rule/law always better than the old? And in this case, there are different codes in effect in different sections of the country. The new tech was simply citing what he was familiar with. But my tank was installed in keeping with the code in my area. So again, which code do you trust? Which expert do you trust?

- **Comment #4.** 'WV' commented:

I got a whump education once years ago. We were out camping and I lit the burner on the stove in our pickup camper to warm some food up. I set the pan on the burner and stepped outside for a minute. When I came back in the camper I noticed the burner was out. I removed the pan so I could light the burner and struck a match, whump. Hair on the arm gone and eyebrows smaller. I am sure the only reason I am still here is because of the gas that got vented out of the camper when I opened the door to get back in it. I now have a very healthy respect for it and always keep a very close eye on it. Since then I have had burners go out on grills and stove several times. Every time I made sure to ventilate enough before trying to re-light to insure I don't even get a poof from it. To date, eyebrows and arm hair remain intact. Lesson learned.